Raphael Santi...

Edward McCurdy

Nabu Public Domain Reprints:

You are holding a reproduction of an original work published before 1923 that is in the public domain in the United States of America, and possibly other countries. You may freely copy and distribute this work as no entity (individual or corporate) has a copyright on the body of the work. This book may contain prior copyright references, and library stamps (as most of these works were scanned from library copies). These have been scanned and retained as part of the historical artifact.

This book may have occasional imperfections such as missing or blurred pages, poor pictures, errant marks, etc. that were either part of the original artifact, or were introduced by the scanning process. We believe this work is culturally important, and despite the imperfections, have elected to bring it back into print as part of our continuing commitment to the preservation of printed works worldwide. We appreciate your understanding of the imperfections in the preservation process, and hope you enjoy this valuable book.

THE ARUNDEL LIBRARY
OF GREAT MASTERS

The Arundel Library of Great Masters

ANTHONY VAN DYCK. A Further Study by Lionel Cust

SANDRO BOTTICELLI. By Adolf Paul Oppé

RAPHAEL SANTI. By Edward McCurdy

LONDON: HODDER AND STOUGHTON

RAPHAEL SANTI
BY EDWARD McCURDY
WITH TWENTY ILLUSTRATIONS IN COLOUR EXECUTED UNDER THE SUPERVISION OF THE MEDICI SOCIETY

HODDER AND STOUGHTON: PUBLISHERS
LONDON AND NEW YORK

Printed in Great Britain 1917 by T. and A. Constable, Edinburgh

CONTENTS

CHAPTER I
ENVIRONMENT 1

CHAPTER II
RECORD 11

CHAPTER III
PERSONALITY 37

CHAPTER IV
PLACE IN ART 54

ACHIEVEMENT.—STUDIED IN CERTAIN EXAMPLES:—

    I. The Vision of a Knight . . . 61
    II. The Madonna Conestabile . . . 68
    III. The Crucifixion 77
    IV. The Marriage of the Virgin (Lo Sposalizio) . 84
    V. The Madonna del Gran Duca . . 91

RAPHAEL SANTI

		PAGE
VI.	The Portrait of Angelo Doni	97
VII.	The Madonna of the Meadow	104
VIII.	The Madonna del Cardellino	111
IX.	The Portrait of Raphael	119
X.	The Madonna of the House of Orleans	124
XI.	S. George	130
XII.	The Entombment	140
XIII.	The Madonna of the House of Alba	149
XIV.	The Parnassus	156
XV.	The Portrait of Julius II	166
XVI.	The Portrait of Baldassare Castiglione	173
XVII.	The Madonna della Sedia	181
XVIII.	The Madonna di San Sisto	188
XIX.	The Portrait of Leo X with the Cardinals Giulio de' Medici and Ludovico de' Rossi	194
XX.	The Portrait of a Lady	201

RAPHAEL SANTI

CHAPTER I

ENVIRONMENT

FIRST as to the Umbrian background,—environment being of much greater import as a creative influence during an artist's youth than in any of the periods of maturity. You find it in all fidelity in the pages of Dennistoun's *Memoirs of the Dukes of Urbino*, where the facts are wrought to such a structure of life as finally to recapture something of its swift vigour and simplicity. You find it in Vespasiano, the Duke Federigo's librarian and biographer, who has preserved something of the high security and lettered ease of the court of the great condottiere; and again as drawn by a master hand in Castiglione's *Courtier*, a 'portrait in painting,' so he styles it, ' of the Court of Urbino: not of the handiwork of Raphael or Michael-Angelo, but of an unknown painter, and that can do no more but draw the principal lines, without setting forth the truth with beautiful colours, or making it appear by the art of Perspective that it is not.'

There is colour fresh with beauty in those descriptions of the scenes amid which, for hours after the Duke Guidobaldo had retired to rest by reason of his infirmities, the Duchess presided over discourses akin in substance to those of the half legendary courts of Provence, 'and not one of them felt any heaviness of sleep in his eyes,' so wise and witty the company there gathered, so keen the passage of opinion. He tells how the assembly which had met to do honour to Pope Julius II. on his way back from Bologna, Bembo, Bibbiena, Giuliano de' Medici, and others only less distinguished, when the Lady Emila Pia, who was endowed with so lively a wit as to seem the mistress and ringleader of all the company, had chosen Fregoso's theme of 'the perfect courtier,' all attempted to define 'all such conditions and particular qualities as of necessity must be in him that deserveth this name.'

How unreal in the scene unfolded in Castiglione's pages was the memory—scarce four years old—of Cæsar Borgia's incursion, of the flight of Guidobaldo and the submission of all his duchy except a few eyrie fortresses to the rule of the invader! Of such contrasts, abrupt as the descent from alp to plain, the Umbrian background is made up.

The first Duke Federigo, whose trade was war, spent in Urbino what he earned elsewhere as captain general of the Italian league. An eager critic of art and a patron, he was captious in his preferences, which serve to indicate the antiquarian bent of his mind. 'To hear him converse with a sculptor,' said Vespasiano, 'you would have thought he was a master of the craft.' 'In painting, too,' he adds, 'he displayed the most acute

ENVIRONMENT

judgment; and as he could not find among the Italians worthy masters of oil colours, he sent to Flanders for one, who painted for him the philosophers and poets and the doctors of the Church. He also brought from Flanders masters in the art of tapestry.' The Duke himself was portrayed with the rest, and appears amid his family, in Flemish fidelity, rather stiff and angular, in the work of Justus of Ghent in the Palace at Urbino, and also in that in the Barberini Palace at Rome. Comparatively few Italian artists visited his court. Among the number were, however, Paolo Uccello, Gentile da Fabriano, and Piero de' Franceschi; the last named having been the guest of Giovanni Santi when he came to Urbino in response to an invitation to paint an altarpiece for the brotherhood of the Corpus Domini. It was on this occasion probably that Piero did the panel portraits of the Duke and the Duchess Battista now in the Uffizi, with triumphs on the reverse side.

Apart from such patronage of art as opportunity offered, Federigo's famous library was 'dukedom large enough' in the life of his desires. Vespasiano extolled it as the superior of any formed within a thousand years. He describes it as having contained copies of all known Greek and Latin authors, of those in Hebrew readily accessible, together with a complete collection of Italian poets, historians and commentators, and treatises on the arts and sciences. The duke's aim was, he says, 'to obtain every book in all branches of learning, ancient and modern, original or translated,' and in pursuance of it his emissaries were at work for upwards of fourteen years, all over Italy and elsewhere, purchasing and transcribing manuscripts, of which alone the library was made up. The palace where these treasures were housed, the library, according to Castiglione, being esteemed its chief ornament, had been built, by the Duke's command, by Luciano de Laurana on the rugged heights of the city. Castiglione extols it as 'in the opinion of many men the fairest that was to be found in all Italy.' He enumerates its silver plate, its hangings of cloth-of-gold and silk, its antique statuary in bronze and marble, its paintings and musical instruments. They were witnesses, like the library, to the taste of its founder, whose impress lent a certain flavour of antiquarianism to the state of culture which prevailed in the city at the time of Guidobaldo.

The whole duchy over which the Montefeltro ruled was but forty miles square. Like its lesser neighbour San Marino perched on its triple peak, Urbino in high security above the wash of the tides of war, 'in a hard and sharp situation,' as Hoby renders it, ensconced amid its gaunt hills, with steep ravines breaking at the base into odorous leafy valleys, lay far apart from the greater roads of passage through Italy. To the Renaissance traveller the ordered quiet of its changeless days may well have seemed as it were one of the last strongholds of mediæval enchantment. As such the city served as the scene of the nascent dream of the youthful Raphael.

To its comparative immunity from the ravages of war is directly to be attributed the fact of Urbino having been

ENVIRONMENT

the painter's birthplace. The records of the family go back to the beginning of the fourteenth century, when a Sante was living at Colbordolo, a small hill-town in the province of Urbino, high above the valley of the Foglia, now a grey mass of farms and old walls. There for upwards of a century the family prospered, until in 1446 Sigismondo Malatesta, in command of the papal troops, pillaged and burned the town for having dared to refuse his followers entrance. The lands of Peruzuolo Santi were laid waste, and apparently the fear that what had happened once might happen again caused him to migrate to Urbino in the year 1450.

There Peruzuolo and his son Sante carried on the business of general traders, and in course of time became possessed of land and of two houses, situated in the Contrada del Monte, in one of which they lived and kept their store. There Giovanni Santi, the son of Sante, worked as a painter and goldsmith, and there somewhat late in life he brought as a bride Magia Ciarla, the daughter of a prosperous tradesman of the city, and their third child, the only one who lived to maturity, was Raphael. Giovanni Santi had broken away from the immemorial occupations of his race; preferring, not without difficulty, as he himself says, the art of painting, when he might have chosen a career which would have insured his future welfare. In the case of Raphael no such difficulty ever existed. The artist's environment, the familiarity with the methods and technique of the painter were his as a birthright.

RAPHAEL SANTI

A certain independent interest attaches to the career of Giovanni Santi. He was one of those lesser craftsmen whose talents traversed a wide field. Altarpieces in plenty when opportunity offered—but he was as ready to paint a banner for a procession, to colour an escutcheon or to gild a candelabra or a crucifix. He also wrote poetry. Had he not been Raphael's father the rounded whole which his life makes, 'toiling hopefully,' would be more readily apparent. Owing in part, no doubt, to Federigo's preference for foreign masters, his more important commissions were executed for the lesser towns of Umbria and the Marches, for Gradara, Cagli, Pesaro, and Fano, and there for the most part they remain, although examples of his art are to be found in the Vatican, the Brera, Berlin, and the National Gallery. Together with that air of quietude and gravity characteristic of all Umbrian art, they possess a simplicity and rough homeliness which form a prelude to the chord of natural feeling played by the art of Raphael, marking an important stage in the divergence from the impressive symbolism of such earlier work as that of Ottaviano Nelli at Gubbio, the natal city of the art of Urbino.

With the death of the Duke Federigo in 1482 the preference for foreign artists at the Montefeltrian court ended, and after the marriage of Guidobaldo to Elisabetta Gonzaga, which took place in 1488, Santi enjoyed an increased measure of patronage.

The young Duchess sat to him for her portrait and

ENVIRONMENT

commissioned him to go to Mantua to paint that of Cardinal Gonzaga. The terms of the letter in which she announced the fact of his death to Isabella d'Este are such as to suggest a close degree of personal interest :—' it is now about three weeks since Giovanni Santi the painter passed away ; he died in full possession of his senses and at peace with all the world, and may God have mercy upon his soul.'

During the later years of his life he had come into relation with the court in the capacity of poet as well as of painter. A masque of his composing, of which the representation lasted for three hours, with over seventy characters, in which Juno and Diana debate the respective merits of the married and single state before Jove and the celestial deities, Jove subsequently giving sentence in favour of Juno, is mentioned in a letter from one of the escort of the young Duchess to her sister Maddalena Gonzaga, as having been acted at Urbino in February 1488 on the occasion of her marriage, the writer promising also to send a copy of it, which he was expecting shortly to receive from the author.

The only other work of which there is record is the *Rhyming Chronicle*, in which he set out to tell in *terza rima* ' the life and glorious deeds of the Duke Federigo '; the undertaking amounting to over twenty-three thousand lines. An edition of it was published twenty-one years ago by Dr. Holtzinger from the unique manuscript in the Vatican. It is dedicated to the Duke Guidobaldo in a modest preface, in which Giovanni Santi makes some reference to the struggles of his life; it is to be inferred from it that he did not take up the career of a painter until a comparatively late period. The debt to Dante is very marked in the vision in the opening cantos of the author's passage through a dark forest beset with foes, and finally his guidance by the shade of Plutarch and converse with famous warriors and the ancestors of his hero. He is of more interest as the simple annalist, despite the prolixity of the narrative and the tendency to exalt every minor engagement to heroic proportions which obscures the due perspective of events.

He had not himself much cause for gratitude to the subject of the poem, but he warmed to his work, and the category of exploits which he obtained from various members of the Duke's household was sufficient to sustain his eulogy.

A closer feeling of personal interest seems to vitalise the long interlude in which, following on his visit to Mantua, he passes in review the work of contemporary painters and sculptors. The supremacy given to Mantegna, to whose work the rest are cited only as a background, is sufficiently to be accounted for by the spectacle of his art which the city of the Gonzagas had afforded him. The list is a comprehensive one, and the omission of the name of Justus of Ghent, the favourite painter of the Duke Federigo, is obviously intentional. His resentment at lack of patronage finds this outlet. Among many terse phrases of description the reference to Melozzo da Forli has a certain individual interest:—

ENVIRONMENT

'Melozzo to me so dear, who has made so great an advance in perspective.' In conjunction with certain stylistic analogies in the work of the two painters, the reference may perhaps throw light on the otherwise obscure question of who the painter was from whom Giovanni Santi received his first lessons in art.

The wide range of artistic sympathies revealed by this section of the *Rhyming Chronicle*, the fondness for mediæval allegory and the use of classical mythology in the prologue, which forms a veritable hymn to the Renaissance, the palpable and reverent debt to Dante, the tendency to moralising, the many passages of description of natural scenery scattered throughout the poem and the fervour with which he recounts the details about the Palace of Urbino—all these serve to make us more acquainted with the personality of Giovanni Santi, and to a corresponding extent they illustrate, as nothing else can, the nature of the influences which encompassed Raphael during his early years.

Tradition tells of his having been the model for an angel in Giovanni Santi's fresco at Cagli. Vasari speaks of Giovanni Santi's resolve that the boy should be brought up under his own eye. It is natural to infer that he was his constant companion in the daily round of his life at Urbino, went with him often to the Palace, and accompanied him on some of his commissions. He would be familiar with the scheme of the poem, and must have taken a special interest in the mythological and artistic portions, which would harmonise most nearly with the nascent dream. From the fact of their names occurring in the latter section he derived his first conception of many of his contemporaries. Perugino, there termed 'a divine painter,' was afterwards his master; Leonardo, whose name is linked with Perugino's, was his chief example during a period of years at Florence; Donatello, Masaccio, Verrocchio are among the names of those he found there, of whose work he learnt as opportunity offered.

Giovanni Santi died when Raphael was eleven years old. The background was as yet little more than an outline, but the lines were functional. Urbino under the Montefeltrian Dukes, its Palace and the life of its court as seen and as mirrored in the pages of the *Rhyming Chronicle*—these are the environment so far as they established it. The literary labours of Giovanni Santi were only less important than his creations as a painter in the part they played in evoking images in the mind of the youthful Raphael.

CHAPTER II

RECORD

THERE is an almost complete dearth of documentary evidence as to the facts of the earlier part of Raphael's life. Even the date of his birth is a matter of inference and deduction. The inscription on his tomb in the Pantheon composed by Bembo, whose intimacy with the painter was such as to establish the truth of the statement, says that he died on the sixth of April, 1520, being exactly thirty-seven years old on that day.

VIXIT · AN · XXXVII · INTEGER · INTEGROS
QVO · DIE · NATVS · EST · EO · ESSE · DESIIT
VIII · ID · APRIL · MDXX.

Marco Antonio Michiel, in a letter written to Venice on the eleventh of April, says the death took place on 'Good Friday.' The sixth of April, 1520, was a Good Friday, and Vasari, following the inscription on the tomb but forgetting that Good Friday was a movable feast, refers to the painter's birth as having occurred on that day in the year 1483, which would be the 26th or 28th of March according as the calculation is made by the astronomical tables or the Julian calendar.

The latter date appears in the majority of modern biographies, following Vasari, but the natural deduction from Bembo's statement is that the painter was born on the 6th of April, 1483.

His mother, Magia Ciarla, died when he was eight years old; his father married again in the following year, and died two years subsequently, at the beginning of August 1494. The fact is alluded to in a letter written by the Duchess Elisabetta to her sister-in-law Isabella d'Este, on the 19th day of August.

Although the fact of Giovanni Santi having died when Raphael was only eleven years old is sufficient of itself to discredit altogether Vasari's account of his having himself placed his son in Perugino's studio, it does not in any way lessen the probability that it was from Giovanni Santi himself, as Vasari states, that Raphael acquired his first instruction in art.

It would be strange if this were not so, for, apart from the story of his having served as a model at Cagli, it is entirely natural to suppose that as a child he accompanied Santi on some of his artistic commissions in Umbria, that he sat in his studio and watched him at his work, that he copied his drawings and helped to mix his colours, and was in fact a pupil to the extent that his years allowed. Despite the chameleon-like quality which characterises the various stages of his art, influence superseding influence continually, there remains a substratum of simplicity and naturalness of feeling in the most ornate of his Madonnas which is apparently directly derived from the homely creations of Santi.

In the April following Santi's death Timoteo Viti

returned to his native city Urbino, after five years of study under Francia at Bologna, and soon after his return Raphael, who had remained in close association with Santi's assistant Evangelista di Pian di Meleto, entered his studio as a pupil or assistant, Viti and Evangelista being afterwards employed together in painting the figures of the Muses for the Ducal Library.

This theory of Raphael having studied under Timoteo Viti owes its inception to Morelli. It bridges over a hiatus in the history of his life as defined by record. The references to him in the will of Giovanni Santi and in the various records of the litigation which followed it concerning the non-payment of the dowry to his step-mother by his uncle the priest, all point to his presence in Urbino for several years after Santi's death. Timoteo Viti on his return from Bologna was by far the most celebrated artist in Urbino, and therefore the most likely for Raphael to have approached. His friendly relations at a later period with Francia, shown by the letter that he wrote to him in which mention is made of an interchange of drawings, are entirely in harmony with the probability of his having studied under Francia's old pupil. But the case really rests entirely on stylistic grounds, and on these it rests as securely as it may. Parallelisms of detail and of general scheme of composition are frequent. The influence of Timoteo, fresh from his long association with Francia, is responsible for the apparently North Italian sobriety of colour and the romanticism of arrangement visible in what are presumably Raphael's earliest works, and in the comparative breadth and robustness of type which showed itself on occasions even after the time of his association with Perugino.

His name first appears in a commission in conjunction with that of Evangelista di Pian di Meleto in a contract for an altarpiece of the coronation of San Nicola da Tolentino for the church of S. Agostino at Città di Castello. The work was in progress from December 1500 to September 1501. Raphael's name occurs first in the contract. He was then seventeen, and already in the year of his birth Evangelista had become his father's assistant. The mere order of the names, coupled with the fact that Evangelista's position in art is utterly insignificant and that no separate commissions can be assigned to him with any certainty, appears conclusive against the supposition which has recently been put forward, that Raphael was for a time in the position of a pupil to Evangelista. The sketches for the composition of the altarpiece at the Wicar Museum at Lille and the fragments of it which have been identified by Dr. Fischel in the Museums at Naples and Brescia offer convincing testimony that Evangelista's share in the composition can only have been a subsidiary one. The silver-point drawing of the head of S. Nicholas and the fragment with God the Father at Naples have a delicacy and refinement which is obviously due to the inspiration of Perugino, while the naturalness and simplicity of the beautiful fragment with the half-length figure of an angel at Brescia shows that the influence of Timoteo Viti was still an important factor, as was in a less degree that of the art of Giovanni Santi.

There is no direct evidence as to the exact time at which Raphael first came into association with Perugino, but a number of circumstances combine to define the date within somewhat narrow limits. Between the years 1493 and 1499 Perugino spent very little time in Perugia. His headquarters were in Florence, where he married in 1493, and where in the following year he bought a house in the Via Pinti.

He was subsequently occupied with commissions in Florence, Venice and Fano. It is quite certain that Raphael could not have been his pupil or assistant during this period, if only because his manner could not then have remained immune from Florentine influences, as it did until after the painting of the Sposalizio in 1504.

In the record of the lawsuit brought in June 1499 by Raphael's step-mother to compel Bartolommeo Santi to observe the provisions of her husband's will, Raphael is referred to as being then in Urbino. When the case came up for settlement in May of the following year, he is stated to be absent.

Early in the year 1499 Perugino left Florence and returned to Perugia to undertake the decoration of the Collegio del Cambio. These frescoes, which are among his most important works, occupied him during the greater part of the years 1499 and 1500, and during this period Raphael joined him in the capacity of an assistant. Perugino's name had been linked with that of Leonardo in a couplet in Giovanni Santi's *Rhyming Chronicle*, and his reputation far exceeded that of any other Umbrian painter. To learn his methods was a natural stage in the continuous development of Raphael's art, which took opportunity as it served, and made itself free of the Umbrian power of feeling and repose before attempting to acquire the enhanced vitality and naturalism which Florentine art revealed.

The magnitude of Perugino's commissions, and the rapidity with which they were executed, are of themselves conclusive of the extent to which his assistants must have shared in their execution, and Raphael's share in the subsidiary portions of the works in the Cambio must have been considerable. Venturi assigns the figure of Fortitude entirely to him, and also the composition on the wall on which God the Father is represented in a *mandorla*, surrounded by angels, with a row of prophets and sibyls standing below. The conclusion is arrived at entirely on stylistic considerations. Contemporary historians and long-continuing tradition assign the whole work to Perugino, and the substantial unity of conception and technique reinforces this verdict. The portions which Venturi ascribes to Raphael would appear to have a freedom and a maturity considerably in excess of what is found in any admitted work by him of this period.

The bestowal in December 1500 upon Raphael and Evangelista di Pian di Meleto of the commission for an altarpiece at Città di Castello may very probably have been due to the friendship which existed between the Vitelli, the rulers of Città di Castello, and the Montefeltrian Dukes of Urbino. It followed immediately after the decoration of the Cambio. The existing fragments of the picture suffice to show the comparative timidity of his independent work, and thereby furnish one of the strongest arguments in favour of the view of tradition that his work in the Cambio was confined to such subsidiary parts as were usually relegated to assistants. It was probably while thus engaged at Città di Castello that the two artists were given the work of painting a processional banner for the Brotherhood of the Trinity which is still preserved in the museum of the town. On one side is the 'Creation of Eve' assigned by Venturi to Evangelista: the work is sufficiently characterless for no one to wish to cavil with the attribution. On the other—that ascribed to Raphael—is a Trinity with Saints Sebastian and Roch kneeling in adoration, the composition of which, as Mr. Herbert Cook has pointed out, presents a close analogy to a 'Trinity' by Timoteo Viti in the Brera Gallery at Milan. The work is curiously reminiscent in technique of Raphael's earlier master.

The completion of these commissions must have been followed by a further period of association with Perugino, whose influence now becomes the dominant one in Raphael's work. The two painters after a time worked upon very equal terms, each making free use in his compositions of the drawings and studies of the other.

RAPHAEL SANTI

As a consequence of this the authorship of certain Madonna pictures of this period is hard to determine with any degree of certainty. So completely had Raphael assimilated the spirit of Perugino's art within three years of his arrival at Perugia as almost to justify the dictum of Vasari, that the altarpiece of the *Crucifixion*, executed at this time for a patron at Città di Castello, and based on numerous drawings by Perugino, is only accepted as his work rather than that of the elder painter because it bears his signature.

Wise with this knowledge afforded us, we may discern points of difference, inceptions which should grow to fruitage and the presence of a profounder feeling for beauty. The *Crucifixion* nevertheless represents the moment of closest approach of the one to the other.

There is by contrast some slight accretion of independent vision in the *Coronation of the Virgin* which he painted for the Oddi chapel in the Cathedral of Perugia, and the *Sposalizio*, a commission for a church in Città di Castello. Both probably were begun in Perugino's studio and based in part upon compositions by him. The *Sposalizio*, which he signed with his name and the date, 1504, marks the limit of his exploration of the world according to Perugino's projection; which was after all a somewhat Mercator-like performance by contrast with what the artist was then beginning to body forth in Florence and elsewhere. But for the tidings of this Raphael might well have continued to multiply altarpieces in Umbria, enhancing the charm of the Peruginesque conception by added structural fidelity, by simplicity, and by the deeper gradation of tones.

According to Vasari, he was induced by Pinturicchio to go to Siena to assist him in the Piccolomini frescoes in the Cathedral Library, and while thus engaged, having in fact made certain of the drawings, he heard such praise of Leonardo's work in Florence that he decided to set out there forthwith. The drawings in question are attributed by Morelli to Pinturicchio himself. Should any of them be deemed to possess Raphaelesque quality it might be considered a free copy of a Pinturicchio original. While the theory of his co-operation in the Piccolomini frescoes is now generally discredited, his association with Pinturicchio at Perugia is established by the fact that certain of the Madonna pictures which he painted at Perugia were founded upon drawings by Pinturicchio, with whom he may have studied during some of Perugino's absences upon commissions.

The frescoes in the Cathedral Library were in progress from 1502 to 1509 and the narrative would suggest that Raphael was there at the inception. This may have been the case, but if so he did not go direct from Siena to Florence. The credibility of the narrative is still further impugned by a reference to the horses in Leonardo's cartoon for the 'Battle of Anghiari' as having formed the special object of attraction which took him to Florence, the said cartoon not having been completed until the beginning of 1505. All that can be inferred from Vasari is that it was the tidings of the progress of art in Florence which snapped the chain of habit that bound him to Perugino.

In the summer of 1504 he seems to have returned to Urbino, and there executed a few commissions, principally of small cabinet pictures, for which the Duke apparently had a special fondness. Towards the end of the year he went to Florence. A letter written by Giovanna della Rovere, the Duchess of Sora and 'Prefetessa di Roma,' dated Urbino, October the first, 1504, commends to the good offices of the Gonfaloniere Piero Soderini the bearer, Raphael, 'a painter of Urbino, who, being gifted with natural talent for art, has decided to spend some time in Florence in order to continue his studies.' The writer refers in affectionate terms to the painter's father as 'an excellent man and very dear to me.'

The fact that in a letter which Raphael wrote from Florence nearly two years later to his uncle in Urbino, he expressed his desire to obtain a letter from the Lord Prefect to the Gonfaloniere, causes one to wonder whether the Prefetessa's letter was ever presented, or whether it failed of its purpose, but in any case the date of it must be very near that at which Raphael went to Florence.

Thereafter follow four years of crowded life in the Tuscan city, by contrast with which the time he had spent in Perugia was as a sojourn in 'the still-vexed Bermoothes.'

These Florentine years are among the richest in achievement of any in the annals of art. Vasari has gathered up the local traditions; has told with some fulness of his coming, eager and impressionable, into the midst of the art world of Florence; of friendships quickly formed; of the indefatigable ardour with which he made the city's heritage his own, both 'the old and the new and everything beautiful.' At sight of her art he who had been a master executing commissions became a pupil once more, studying 'the old things of Masaccio' in the Carmine, and the creations of Michelangelo and Leonardo; and desiring especially to attain what he saw revealed in the work of the two last, he set himself new schemes of study involving deeper researches into principles and natural forms. Fra Bartolommeo is cited among the number of his intimate friends; Vasari tells how he sought to acquire his method of colouring, and in exchange taught him his perspective. As a consequence of these studies his work, we are told, underwent so extraordinary a change and development that it might be considered to be by another hand.

It is a vision of tireless activity, revealing indefatigable concentration of purpose; yet the actual record, as established by the evidence of works unmistakably of this period, is more varied than Vasari's presentment. Not only to those masters whom Vasari mentions had he put himself to school, but—as his paintings and sketches reveal—to Donatello, to Pollaiuolo, to Ghirlandaio, to Signorelli, and to Mantegna, laying the work of each in turn under tribute, wresting from it some rule of method, some power of precision of line or depth of colour, some standard of quality or grace.

Michelangelo had finished the 'David,' and was at work on the great cartoon for the Signoria of the 'Pisan

RAPHAEL SANTI

Soldiers Bathing,' in which the treatment of the nude was a revealment of unexampled power of modelling. Leonardo, who was the chief god of his idolatry, whom, according to Vasari, he accounted greater than all others in the power to render grace and movement, had finished the 'Mona Lisa,' and his work on the 'Anghiari' cartoon was nearing completion. Around the first of these Raphael must have hovered continually, as a moth round a candle, before he painted the portrait of *Maddalena Doni*, the sketch for which in the Louvre stands for a record of the singeing of wings in the hazardous quest. Drawings serve also to show with what zeal he strove to recapture the swift, flame-like movement of the combatants in the cartoon of the 'Battle of Anghiari.'

In all his portraits of this period there is as much of Leonardo's super-subtle modelling as he could compass, oddly blended with something of the structural simplicity and directness of Ghirlandaio, and his debt is also readily obvious in such a work as the *S. George*, where the composition is derived from Donatello, while in certain altarpieces and in that fresco of the Trinity in S. Severo which he went to Perugia in order to paint, the influence of Fra Bartolommeo is equally perceptible. Side by side with such evidence of sedulous apprenticeship is the new phenomenon presented by the steady growth of self-contained power of his Madonna pictures, in which his individuality always seemed to find comparatively unfettered utterance. The greater number of these works, to which he owes his unique position as the painter of the central motive of Christian art, were produced during these four years in Florence. While these reveal in fulness the measure of his absorption in the influences amid which he was placed,—the progression from the *Madonna del Gran Duca* to the *Cardellino* and the *Madonna in the Meadow* being eloquent of this,—they possess no less a basic unity, the elements of which they were compounded having lain molten as in a crucible in the artist's creative thought.

The course of the Florentine years was broken in upon by visits to Perugia and Urbino, during which Raphael was engaged upon commissions. With that to Perugia, which extended from early in the latter half of the year 1505 until the following spring, four important works are associated. The large altarpiece formerly in the convent of S. Antonio, and now, after many wanderings, in the Pierpoint-Morgan Collection at New York, which bears the date 1505, is so purely Peruginesque in feeling and composition as regards the upper portion that Crowe and Cavalcaselle seem to offer the most natural explanation of its origin by the suggestion that it had been begun before Raphael went to Florence, and the necessity of completing it may have been one of the reasons of his visit to Perugia. The ampler, more statuesque manner of the draperies and bolder treatment of the figures of the saints around the Madonna breathe Florentine influence, which is no less clearly absent in the lunette.

Less conclusive by far is the application of this same theory to the origin of the *Ansidei Madonna*, painted for the Ansidei chapel in the church of S. Fiorenzo at Perugia, for the reason that the work possesses far greater unity. It bears the date 1506, and was therefore either finished during his visit to Perugia or after his return to Florence. It is an Umbrian conception, painted with wider knowledge. Pater defines it happily as 'a specimen of the city's own old art.' 'The kind of thing,' he says, 'that people there had already seen so many times, but done better, in a sense not to be measured by degrees, with a wholly original freedom and life and grace, . . . better as a whole, because better in every minute particular, than ever before.'

The points in which the earlier Perugian manner is predominant—the modelling of the head of the Virgin, the plumpness of the child, the ecstatic expression of the Baptist and the position of his feet, the cast of the draperies and the frequent use of gold—all serve to show how lightly old memories sleep, how the presence of old scenes created a natural recrudescence of sympathy with Umbrian ideals, so impressionable ever was his art.

He painted also while at Perugia, in 1505 as an inscription records, that fresco of the Trinity in S. Severo, which—entirely Umbrian in feeling, but with the arrangement revealing his close intimacy with the work and teaching of Fra Bartolommeo—prefigures also the later triumph of space composition of the *Disputa*.

While engaged upon these works at Perugia he was invited by Donna Atalanta Baglioni to paint an altarpiece for a memorial chapel to her son in the church of

RECORD

S. Francesco. Vasari speaks of his being obliged to return to Florence, but leaving Donna Atalanta with the promise to execute the commission when opportunity offered. The subject chosen was the Entombment, as symbolical of the mother's sorrow. The numerous drawings connected with it reveal him, in the intervals of painting Madonnas, engaging upon new apprenticeships, preparing himself by a deeper study of the laws of structure and the principles of movement, as interpreted in the art of Mantegna and Michelangelo, to render forms whose every action should reveal the stress of passion and movement.

The visit to Urbino, which took place in the autumn of the year following that to Perugia, was a passing back to a serener air. He did a few commissions there, small Madonna pictures, and portraits of the Duke Guidobaldo and of Pietro Bembo, of both of which record ceases at the outset. The court dwelt in new-found security; Castiglione has defined how pleasantly. It was a centre of the arts again; and Raphael's second picture of *S. George*—gartered as the Duke himself had recently become—may well have celebrated the passing away of the Borgian peril. He wrote to his uncle in Urbino on the 21st of April 1508, signing himself Raphael, Painter in Florence.

The letter to Francia, which bears the date the 5th of September of the same year, was written from Rome, he being then much occupied in the service of a patron (Julius II.). These two letters contain all that is known as to the time and circumstances of his departure from

Florence to Rome. A passage in the first letter, in which he requests his uncle to enlist the good offices of the new Duke on his behalf with Pier Soderini, the Gonfaloniere of Florence, who has the power to give a certain commission, is significant as illustrating the difficulty that he experienced in obtaining commissions on a scale commensurate with his ambitions. Like Leonardo, who some twenty-five years previously had left Florence for Milan at the age of thirty, having been given no adequate opportunity of expressing his powers, so Raphael had obtained only private commissions. These had sufficed him only for so long as was necessary in order to learn what he could from the art of the Florentine masters; and that had been done. The thought of the larger surfaces, presenting greater opportunities for the display of power of composition and arrangement, must have been present in his mind since his work at S. Severo at Perugia, and in the letter to Urbino he is seen preparing to claim his due share in the disposition of these works. To the young Duke it would seem, no doubt, that his influence to obtain such commissions would be employed to more effect with his uncle, the Rovere Pope, than with the Gonfaloniere of Florence. So it came about that within a few months of the date of the letter, perhaps indirectly as the result of it, Raphael was in Rome in the Pope's service. Vasari attributes the fact of the Pope giving him employment to the suggestion of his fellow-townsman, Bramante. Julius II. may very possibly have been prompted from both quarters. His projects of decoration in the Vatican were of such magnitude as to draw to Rome all, with a few exceptions, of the most famous of contemporary artists. That under these circumstances Raphael should have immediately obtained important work points to the probability that influence was exerted on his behalf. With the completion of the first of the works, however, his position was secure. Thenceforward, for the remainder of his life, while Michelangelo reigned in the Sistine, all the monumental painting in the Palace of the Vatican was either the work of Raphael himself, or was executed by his assistants from his designs or under his general supervision. The two later stages entirely superseded the first about a year after the death of Julius II., when the painter became more entirely immersed in the multifarious duties which his successor heaped upon him.

His degree of absorption at the outset in the work in the Stanza della Segnatura, and the Pope's insistence, may be inferred from his letter to Francia. Vasari, with some suspicion of legend, speaks of the Pope's delight in the first work which Raphael executed causing him to order the destruction of the work of other painters, old and new, so that he might have a clear field. This same fate befell some of Perugino's work in the Sistine; but what were the works which perished to make way for Raphael's is not recorded. An inscription in the Stanza itself gives 1511 as the date of the completion of the works. In the medallions in the ceiling, which were no doubt painted first, the four allegorical figures of Theology, Poetry, Philosophy, and Law serve as the keynotes of the frescoes below, and by their position symbolise the essential unity of the conception. In the corners of the ceiling between the arches are four scenes emblematical of the arts thus personified; the subjects of these are *The Fall, Apollo and Marsyas, Astronomy* —a figure looking at a globe,—and the *Judgment of Solomon*; while on the walls below are the *Disputa*, the *School of Athens*, and on the two of which the surface is broken by the projection of a window, the *Parnassus* and three allegorical figures representing virtues, with two scenes in which Justinian and Gregory IX. are granting codes of Law.

There is a natural priority in the subjects on the ceiling and the *Disputa*. They have most in common with the spirit of Florentine art. The others reveal more of the freedom of the antique, which gives an ageless vitality to the classicism of the *School of Athens* and the *Parnassus*. It is seen in the easy carriage of the figures and the all-pervading sense of light and air which characterises them. Although this same quality is conspicuous in the *Disputa*, its composition has by contrast something of the formalism of Quattrocento art, of which it is, in fact, the apotheosis, in that it epitomises the essential teaching of the Church of the Middle Ages more vividly and with greater completeness than any other work.

The coming of naturalism is visible in the *Disputa*,

in the fact of the disappearance of the symbols of the Evangelists, and in the diversity of the action while entirely subordinate to the central idea. It reigned supreme in Olympian air in the *School of Athens* and the *Parnassus*. It is seen seeking its inevitable outlet in the realism of portraiture in the scenes with Justinian and Gregory IX. Such union of pure decorative effect, with intellectual strength and breadth of vision as the works in the Stanza della Segnatura possess, is found otherwise in Renaissance art only in Michelangelo's work in the Sistine Chapel.

The more purely historical compositions painted by Raphael between 1511 and 1514, in the room called after the first the Stanza of Heliodorus, were chosen as examples of how the divine protection had been exercised over the Church. The subjects are: *The Expulsion of Heliodorus from the Temple*, the *Miracle of the Mass of Bolsena*, the *Repulse of Attila from Rome by Pope Leo I.*, and the *Liberation of S. Peter*. They reveal the change which Rome witnessed in the spirit of his art as potently as does the *Madonna della Sedia* by contrast with the Florentine prototypes. The power of space composition is undiminished, but he has now become a realist, interested primarily in the world as it is. There is a marked increase in vigour of dramatic presentment, as in the figure of Pope Julius and that of the avenging angel in the *Heliodorus*, while the added colour sense and fidelity of portraiture, which are the distinguishing characteristics of his Roman period, reach their height in the *Mass of Bolsena*, where, for example in the group of Swiss guards, a Venetian richness and depth of colour clothes the firmness of Florentine structure in indissoluble harmony. Only of these two out of the four works in the Stanza can it be said that Raphael had any extensive share in the execution. In that representing the meeting of Leo I. and Attila, which was not completed until after the election of Leo X., whose lineaments consequently appear for those of his predecessor, only the group of the Pope and the cardinals is considered to be by Raphael's own hand, while that of the *Liberation of S. Peter*, with the marvellous effect of the light radiating from the figure of the angel and falling on the armour of the sleeping sentries, which in its impressive simplicity recalls the creations of Piero de' Franceschi, is in execution entirely the work of assistants. For the decoration of the third of these state apartments, in progress from 1514 to 1517, known as the Stanza del Incendio from the *Fire in the Borgo* having been the first subject executed there, the cartoons were made by assistants, and Raphael's share consisted only in suggestion and in a few studies of nude figures for those escaping in the *Fire in the Borgo*, which show something of the same freedom and suppleness of limb as are revealed in the *Galatea*.

Raphael's work in painting in Rome, apart from that of the decoration of the rooms in the Vatican in which his individual share grew steadily less, falls readily into three main groups. The first, consisting of the Madonna pictures, forms a natural continuation of his work in Florence. He was pursuing certain parallel lines of development in the relation of the figures to each other, which were independent of locality. *The Madonna of the House of Alba* on stylistic grounds must be adjudged the earliest. The *Madonna di Foligno* was a commission from the Pope's chamberlain, Sigismondo Conti, who is introduced kneeling as a votary. His death in February 1512 supplies a precise time reference for the date of the picture. The wooded landscape with the town of Foligno and the thunderbolt in the sky is so entirely in the manner of Dosso Dossi, whose apprenticeship to Raphael is a matter of record, as to render certain a date by which it had commenced. Such participation is soon in evidence in all but the greatest of his commissions, creating thereby a varying standard of quality. The figures in the *Madonna di Foligno* show a stage in the progress towards that depth and glow of colour of which the *Madonna della Sedia*, which is about four years later in date of composition, furnishes the supreme example.

The *Madonna di San Sisto*, of approximately the same period, is by contrast more akin in spirit to the earlier work; like the fresco of the *Disputa* in the Stanza della Segnatura, it is charged with the quietude and the idealism of Umbrian feeling.

The fresco of the *Galatea*, painted in the Villa Farnesina in the year 1514, the knowledge of the date being derived from a reference to it contained in a letter from Raphael to Baldassare Castiglione, occupies a position almost by itself among the works of Raphael, in that in it the freedom of the antique which he won by the opportunities of study that Rome afforded finds complete expression; so complete as to endow the spirit of the myth with a joyous self-subsistent vitality. The earlier stages of the study of the antique which he approached with ardour in his first years at Rome have found record in the numerous bas-reliefs and statues in the works in the Stanza della Segnatura, and in the studies of antique statuary in which he found motives for various figures. Casts of bas-reliefs in the Museum of the Capitol point to a like origin for the composition of the *Galatea*, but the result is nevertheless perfect freedom of life and movement.

How ideally graceful, how magnificently conceived, is the figure of *Galatea*, with head half turned and red peplum streaming in the wind, standing in her car curbing the dolphins who draw it across the sea, while Tritons and nymphs are sporting joyously around, and cupids floating in the air above are about to transfix her with their darts!

The third of the groups, into which the Roman work apart from that in the Vatican naturally falls, is that of the portraits. The quickening of the impulse of realism, which all the circumstances of Raphael's life at Rome were calculated to foster, found a natural outlet in the art of portraiture, and here his art underwent most change during the Roman period. It gained in richness and depth of colour from the influence of Venetian work; the study of the antique is responsible for a certain increase in directness and strength of modelling. Devolution to assistants was less extensive of necessity in portrait commissions than in altarpiece and fresco, and so in Raphael's later years the former present the most uniform standard of attainment, and their perfection of technique have established them above the wash of the tides of art criticism.

To this period belong the portraits of *Julius II.* and *Leo X. with two Cardinals*, of a *Cardinal* now in the Prado, of *Tommaso Inghirami*, Prefect of the Vatican Library, transported recently from Volterra to Boston, of *Bindo Altoviti* at Munich, of *Castiglione*, the double portrait of *Navagero* and *Beazzano* in the Doria-Pamphili, the *Giuliano de' Medici* in a private collection at Berlin. The description given in a letter by Bembo of a portrait of the poet *Tebaldeo*, shows that other masterpieces have perished. The portraits of women are curiously infrequent. That known as *La Fornarina* in the Barberini Palace is a triumph of realism, but it is more of the nature of a figure subject than a portrait. The *Donna Velata* in the Pitti Palace stands practically alone. It is an exquisite harmony of grey and gold, a fit pair to the portrait of Castiglione in its quietude and subtility of rendering.

It is in these works, where friendship's bond was most intimate, that the painter's touch seems most facile and penetrative; but in the whole series of Roman portraits—popes, cardinals, and men of letters—types of a ripe humanism rendered with entire sympathy and understanding, he left such a body of work as suffices to establish his rank as one of the few really great portrait-painters of the Renaissance.

During the later years of Raphael's life in Rome, the time which might have been given to art was continually being circumscribed by the multifarious duties that the Pope heaped upon him.

On the death of Bramante in March 1514, precisely a year after the election of Leo X., Raphael was appointed to succeed him as architect of the fabric of S. Peter's.

Passages in letters written during the same year to Castiglione and Simone Ciarla reveal how seriously he entered upon the duties of the position, and how heavily at times he felt its obligations.

In the following year he was appointed by the Pope to the post of inspector of all the antiquities of Rome, and his conception of his duties extended even to the directing of excavations. In a document in the archives of the Capitol, of July 1518, cited by Crowe and Cavalcaselle, his name appears as claiming a statue on behalf of the Pope from the heirs of a certain Gabriel de' Rossi.

On internal evidence he is presumed to have been the author, with some assistance from his friend Castiglione, of a compendious report on all the antiquities of Rome drawn up for presentation to Leo X., which, from the statement of the writer having spent eleven years in Rome, is assigned to the year 1519. It proposed the measuring of all the existing portions of ancient buildings in order to attempt an ideal reconstruction of the city.

RECORD

His presence in Florence is recorded in November 1515 as one of a concourse of artists summoned by Leo X. to advise as to his project of a façade for S. Lorenzo, which, however, Michelangelo persuaded his Holiness to entrust to him alone. In this same month a house in the Via Sistina was purchased on his behalf in his absence, and two years later he acquired the Palazzo Caprini where Bramante had lived. In a letter, bearing a date in November 1516, a correspondent of Michelangelo's warns him to look to his laurels, because Raphael had made a model in clay of a child for Piero d'Ancona, who had almost finished it in marble. 'They say,' he adds, 'it is a very good work.'

There are reports also of other projects in architecture, palaces and villas planned and executed, in addition to the work on the fabric of S. Peter's.

It is hardly surprising that the cartoons of the Acts of the Apostles for the tapestries designed for the Sistine Chapel should be the work of assistants, or that this should also be the case with the series of scenes from the Old and New Testament, popularly known as Raphael's Bible, executed in the Loggie of the Vatican in 1518 and 1519. So also for the Cupid and Psyche series in the Farnesina he supplied only a few of the drawings. Unwilling, however, perhaps that he should be judged by the work of assistants, he set himself, according to Vasari, to execute with his own hand a commission from Cardinal Giulio de' Medici for an altarpiece which should represent the Transfiguration. He had completed the upper portion of

RAPHAEL SANTI

the picture, which ranks with his greatest works, when he was suddenly attacked by fever, acquired as it is believed while following the progress of the excavations. He died, after a week's illness, on the sixth of April 1520, that being the thirty-seventh anniversary of his birth.

CHAPTER III

PERSONALITY

PRODIGALITY of achievement acts somewhat as a veil to personality in the records of the high Renaissance. It was not a time especially rich in memoirs. With the artist, labours of record were a superfluity if he lived in his work, which was his ultimate self; lacking this distinction, they were a thing supererogant. As regards the self more immediate, few biographies are found to possess the vitalising touch that comes from actual intercourse. Those of Raphael are not of the number. Such personalia as have survived the intervening centuries seem curiously few, when we consider the immediate greatness of his fame. An anecdote, possibly apocryphal, preserves a phrase, or an inscription occurs on a drawing sent as friendship's offering,—these possess an additional interest by reason of the tenuity of material. He is genial, courtly, debonair in the relations thus revealed, ever too ready to learn of another's example to feel aught of envy in his performance. It would seem as though the ingrained surliness of disposition which writes itself into all records of Michelangelo found but little cause for outlet in the association of the two.

RAPHAEL SANTI

A glimpse—tantalizingly brief—of the way in which some of his few days of leisure were spent, is afforded by the passage in a letter written by Bembo at Rome in April 1516 to Cardinal Bibbiena at Fiesole, in which he speaks of a visit about to be paid to Tivoli, where his companions are to be the poets Navagero and Beazzano and also Baldassare Castiglione and Raphael. They will, he says, see the old and the new and everything that is beautiful in the place.

The fidelity of long-continued friendship is seen in the recurrence, in this list of companions of his Roman days, of the names of those with whom he had first been brought into association at Urbino at the court of Guidobaldo. Bembo and Castiglione were of that circle who, in the presence of the Duchess Elisabetta, made discourse upon all courtly qualities; with whom, renewing debate in the more spacious air of the Campagna, he set out to see 'the old and the new and everything that is beautiful.' The words serve to suggest something of the range of his intellectual sympathies. They illuminate the broad humanism which went to the making of the compositions in the Stanza della Segnatura, where he stood both for Christ and Apollo in that reconcilement which supreme art affords. These works reveal most potently that kinship of purpose with the art of literature which the record of his friendships helps to establish. Amidst the limbo of lost things is a letter, once in the possession of Count Carlo del Pozzo, in which Raphael asked advice of Ariosto as to what characters should be introduced into these compositions.

PERSONALITY

Some thought derived perhaps from Petrarch's *Triumphs* in the inception, some help in detail from the author of the *Orlando Furioso*, counsel from Castiglione and others—all serve to show how the two arts are co-ordinated in his work in the Segnatura, which forms probably the most compendious interpretation of the complex spirit of the Renaissance.

A few sonnets show this sympathy seeking a more direct expression. One of these appropriately is found on a sheet of studies for the *Disputa*. The theme of the lover's dolours and transports is common enough, and Raphael's utterance never advanced beyond the stage of bondage to rudiments. Although he wears his fetters bravely, adding a list of rhyme words ready for use as the Muse may direct, it all seems a somewhat meticulous pastime in its juxtaposition to the freedom and mastery of technique of the drawing for the *Disputa*.

But the written word affords a more direct revealment of self than is seen in any of Raphael's artistic works.

Letters, as possessing something of the intimacy of direct speech, are of primary importance in the study of personality. From these quite as much as from the published works is derived that indefinable fragrance which attaches to the memory of certain names in literature. Essays, indeed, partake somewhat of the same quality; such, that is, as are a revealment of self only in design a shade more conscious than that of letters, as are those of Montaigne, who could say in preface with complete truth, 'Je suis moy mesme la matière de mon livre.'

RAPHAEL SANTI

The number of Raphael's letters now in existence is four—far fewer than those either of Leonardo da Vinci or Michelangelo, with which comparison is naturally made. All are alike in that they are a direct revealment of self. Those of Leonardo, containing, in addition to complete drafts, many fragments, are almost all without exception addressed to his patrons, the greater part being to Ludovic Sforza. Some breathe his superb confidence of spirit, and reveal, as nothing else does, the heights to which his aspirations soared. Others tell with eloquent brevity of the shifts of penury, of 'works of fame' abandoned of necessity, his own salary being long in arrears and his assistants clamouring to be paid. There is something of the same strain perceptible in Michelangelo's letters, although their nature is more varied, and they are far richer in biographical and historical interest. He, too, like Leonardo, had his tragedy of a monument, that of Pope Julius, bound to which he says of himself that he has lost all his youth. There is the same impatience of the irksome restraint of patrons, together with proof of a more iron will and mordant humour; there is also the grudging malice which could find to say of Raphael more than twenty years after his death, that he had acquired all that he had of art from Michelangelo himself.

How eminently practical, how entirely genial by contrast, are the letters of Raphael!

Two of the four are addressed to an uncle at Urbino, Simone di Battista Ciarla—dear to him as a father, as the

PERSONALITY

opening words express. They show a strong feeling of personal attachment, as do also the epistles to Francia and Baldassare Castiglione. The letters reveal more potently than anything else the amiability, the ready sympathy, the courtesy and happy practicality of his nature.

The occasion of the earliest, written from Florence in April 1508, is the tidings of the death of Guidobaldo.

'I received your letter,' he begins, 'acquainting me with the death of our most illustrious Lord Duke. May God have mercy upon his soul. Truly I could not read your letter without tears. But he is gone, and there is no help for it; we must have patience and resign ourselves to the will of God.' He proceeds in an eminently practical strain to unfold a budget of commissions, all concerning matters in which Simone may help his career:—

He asks him to remind his uncle the priest (Bartolommeo Santi) to send him the panel which served as a covering for the *Madonna of the Prefetessa* (Giovanna della Rovere), as he has not yet sent it; and also to inform him in case any one should be on the point of setting out from Urbino to Florence, since it is important for him to be in a position to satisfy the lady's wishes as he may presently require her help; also to ask Bartolommeo and his aunt Santa, if the Florentine Taddeo Taddei, of whom they have often spoken together, should come to Urbino to spare no expense to do him honour; and he requests Simone Ciarla himself also to show him every possible kindness, because he (Raphael) is under greater obligations to him than to any one else alive.

He goes on to utter some commercial wisdom about a picture upon which he is then engaged, having at the time finished the cartoon. He is unwilling to put a price upon it because he expects to get more by having it valued, and when this has taken place he promises to let Simone Ciarla know the result. The patron who has ordered it has also, he says, promised him other commissions in Florence and in France amounting altogether to three hundred ducats.

He concludes by expressing his great desire to obtain a letter of recommendation from the Lord Prefect to the Gonfaloniere of Florence, because the latter has the power of bestowing the work of the decoration of a certain room. He has already written a few days previously to the same effect to his uncle the priest, and to a certain Giacomo da Roma. If Simone Ciarla will only inform the Prefect for whom it is that his services are invoked, then he is sure that he will accede to the request of his old servant and friend who sends him a thousand remembrances.

So the letter, which commences with trite reflections on the decease of the Duke Guidobaldo, ends with a lively interest in his successor, whose help he invokes to further his fortunes.

The letter lays bare the writer's practical commonsense and extraordinary assiduity of purpose. No stone apparently was ever left unturned which might open out the pathway to success, and the opportunities which came to him so rapidly were in a sense self-created by his

PERSONALITY

quiet pertinacity. His nature was gentle and amiable. He made no enemies. His friendships, which were many, were all brought into association with his work. He built upon firm foundations. He was of Urbino. He looked to be furthered by the patronage of her princes; and his relatives at home, whose good offices might effect this, were kept well acquainted with the nature of his artistic projects.

A note or fragment of a letter of about the same date on the reverse of a sketch for a *Holy Family*, now in the Wicar Museum at Lille, sent by Raphael to an old fellow-pupil, Domenico Alfani, and used by the latter for an altarpiece at Perugia, presents a signal instance of how friendship was association in work:—

'Remember, Domenico,' he says, 'to send me the stanzas of Ricciardo about the tempest which he met with on his journey, and to remind Cesarino to send me that sermon, and give him my greetings. Remember also to urge Donna Atalanta to send me the money, and see that it is in gold, and ask Cesarino also to remind her and to urge her, and if I can do anything else for you let me know.'

The tempest which Ricciardo met with on his journey has been identified by Grimm as an allusion to the twentieth canto of Pulci's *Morgante Maggiore*. For what purpose Raphael required it is unknown. Cesarino was a famous metal-worker at Perugia. The request for money refers presumably to amounts paid by Donna Atalanta Baglioni during the time that Raphael was preparing the *Entombment* for the memorial chapel to her son.

Passavant suggests a possible direct connection between the letter to Simone Ciarla and Raphael's departure for Rome, which took place a few months afterwards. If the young Duke's good offices were invoked, and as to this the persistency revealed in the letter removes any doubt, he may very possibly have thought that he could do more for the painter by approaching his own kinsman, Julius II., who was embarking upon vast schemes of decoration in the Vatican, than by a letter to the Florentine Gonfaloniere. His recommendation may in this case have gone to supplement that of Bramante, of which Vasari makes mention.

The letter from Raphael to Francia, the authenticity of which has been called in question on very slight grounds, first published in 1678 in *Felsina Pittrice* by Malvasia, who discovered it among the Lambertini papers at Bologna, serves as a landmark in the chronology, as forming the earliest evidence of his presence in Rome.

It forms an admirable example of the genial nature of Raphael's relations with his fellow artists. Francia was the older by more than thirty years, and having been the master of Timoteo Viti may be considered to have had some indirect influence in forming Raphael's earliest manner. There is reason to suppose that Raphael visited Bologna from Florence and painted a picture for Bentivoglio, and so made Francia's acquaintance, and when the elder painter, in fulfilment of a promise made between

PERSONALITY

them, perhaps on this same occasion, sent him a present of his portrait, he replied in these words:—

'Dear Messer Francesco,—I have just received your portrait, brought to me by Bazzotto in excellent condition and without any damage, for which I thank you most heartily. It is most beautiful, and so life-like that at times I deceive myself into believing that you are with me and that I hear you speak. I entreat you to have compassion and to excuse the long delay in sending you my own, which, on account of my heavy and incessant labours, I have been prevented from drawing with my own hand according to our agreement; and while I might have sent you one done by one of my assistants and retouched by myself, this did not seem fitting, although it would have served as an acknowledgment of the fact that I cannot equal your work. I pray you to forgive me since you know well what it is to be deprived of your liberty, and to live at the beck and call of patrons and all that this means. I send you in its stead by the same messenger, who is returning in six days' time, another drawing of a Nativity, very different as you will see from the one which I finished and which you were pleased to praise so highly, as indeed you have all my works, so that I feel myself now blushing for this trifle, which you will value more as a token of respect and affection than for any other reason. If in exchange I may receive a drawing of your 'Judith' I shall place it among my dearest and most treasured possessions. Monsignor the Datary is anxiously expecting his little Madonna and

Cardinal Riario his large one, as you will hear more fully from Bazzotto. I also shall view them with that delight and satisfaction which I have felt at all your other Madonnas, never having seen any by any one else which were more beautiful, more devotional, or better executed. Be of good courage, make use of your accustomed prudence, and be assured that I feel your afflictions as though they were my own. Continue to love me as I love you, with all my heart.—ROME, *The 5th Day of September*, 1508.'

The reason he gives for not having fulfilled his promise to Francia, namely, that he is deprived of liberty and at the beck and call of a patron, can only have reference to his employment under Julius II. Five years of almost incessant work under that pontiff and one under his successor intervene between the letter to Francia and that to Baldassare Castiglione, which, from the reference that it contains to his appointment as architect of S. Peter's, may be assigned to the year 1514, the year of the second letter to Simone Ciarla.

There is a certain mellowness perceptible in it. A confident tone arises naturally from the fact of his triumphant success. He seems to have something of the joy in life of one to whom all its gifts are golden, something also of the satiety. Painting is no longer his sole or even apparently his chief employment in the Pope's service. He speaks gravely of the burdensome nature of his various occupations, especially in connection with his appointment as architect of S. Peter's. In connection apparently

PERSONALITY

with the office he held of conservator of ancient buildings in Rome, he expresses his desire to investigate the laws of beauty in their construction, although the attempt, he fears, may prove but a flight of Icarus. The reference to the *Galatea*, which serves to define the date of the composition of the fresco, is steeped in courtier-like phrases of submission and deference to the judgment of his friend Castiglione in matters of æsthetics. Through these, as through a thin veil of metaphor, appear the outlines of the theory which Raphael held as to the relations which should exist in the artist's conception between the actual and the ideal. It is a pretty piece of Platonism. 'To paint a beautiful woman one must see many.' But as there is no certainty of the fair prospect enduring, he comes to prefer the *certa idea* which the artist carries with him and toils to reproduce, creating thus a type of beauty independent alike of model or of critic, who are of necessity rare when of excellence. The theory is of tenfold more significance as giving an insight into his method. He might say of himself as did Dürer in reference to his writings on the theory of art: 'Whatever I have set down with the pen I have done with the hand.'

'My Lord Count,' the letter runs, 'I have made several drawings of the subject which your Highness suggested, and they give pleasure to all who see them unless all conspire to flatter me, but I do not satisfy my own judgment because I doubt my satisfying yours. I now send them to your Highness, and beg you to make a selection of them if you think any worthy of your acceptance. Our Lord (the Pope) while conferring an honour upon me has placed a great burden on my shoulders, namely, the care of the fabric of S. Peter's. I hope I shall not sink under it, and I hope this the more because the model which I have made pleases his Holiness and has been praised by many persons of fine judgment. But my thoughts rise higher. I wish to discover the principles of beauty in the forms of ancient buildings, and I do not know whether my flight will not be like that of Icarus. Vitruvius gives me some light, but not as much as I require.

'Concerning the *Galatea*, I should consider myself a great master if it possessed half the merits of which you write me; but I recognise in your words the love that you bear to me. In my opinion, in order to paint a beautiful woman one must see many; with this further condition, that your Highness must be with me to choose which is the fairest.

'But since there is a dearth both of good judges and of beautiful women, I follow a certain ideal which comes into my mind. Whether or no this has in it any artistic excellence I cannot tell, but I strive to attain to it.

'I await your Highness' commands.

'From Rome.'

This epistolary sequence, which presents a more finished picture of Raphael's personality than is obtainable from any other source, is ended by the second letter to Simone Ciarla. It bears the date the first of July, 1514. Whether it is actually earlier or later than that

PERSONALITY

to Castiglione is impossible to decide, but from the more familiar nature of the friendship with the uncle, 'dearest in the place of a father' as before, the self-portrait is more intimate. The contents—a budget of gossip where they touch events—show very clearly the effect upon the temperament of the painter of his six years of great commissions in Rome. In lieu of the suggestions and petitions of the earlier letter to Simone, all centering round the subject of his career as an artist, with regard to which in small ways Simone Ciarla may be useful, there is the confidence born of attainment, and mingling with the old affection which, as often, expresses itself in part in raillery, there is just a touch of hauteur in explaining why the correspondence has now come to be irregular. Simone's letter is most dear to him as showing that he is not offended by his silence. This would, he adds, be unreasonable, because it is tiresome to have to write when one has nothing of any importance to say. Later on in a passage rather contradictory to this, because it shows that Simone has in fact expressed his annoyance, he says that the reproaches ought rather to come from him, because Simone sits all day long pen in hand and yet has let six months pass without writing. As, however, he has now raised an important question, Raphael promises to put him in possession of his views upon it as fully as possible. The question is no less a one than that of the painter's marriage; his uncle having apparently on a former occasion urged him to marry and come to live at Urbino, has reverted to the subject, and therefore Raphael explains his position with regard to matrimony.

RAPHAEL SANTI

There is a frank materialism about it. The industrious apprentice of the old story who married his master's daughter was not more level-headed and calculating in his relations with the fair sex than this painter of Madonnas shows himself to be.

When Leonardo postulates the desirability of a life of solitude for the artist it is in order that the mind may move more freely in its work of creation. Raphael congratulates himself upon having remained single apparently because he has been enabled as a consequence to save money and buy property.

There are tales of mistresses in Vasari—common enough in the annals of the artists of the Renaissance. It were ill to judge the morality of the relationship thus implied by the name. But whoever they were he was quite ready to throw them over. Money and position, these were better for him than marriage. But might he not unite them all ! In a subsequent passage he is seen prepared to angle somewhat after the manner of the manœuvring parent in the play,—but with his own hand for bait. Would that one might think he was merely writing nonsense calculated to amuse a garrulous and gossip-loving old man with whom apparently he had had some estrangement ! But the tale is altogether too circumstantial to be thus lightly dismissed, and in so far as it relates to the niece of Cardinal Bibbiena it is corroborated by Vasari. It was in the sumptuous decoration of Cardinal Bibbiena's bathroom that it is recorded Raphael frittered away some of the creative energy of his later

PERSONALITY

years. The sections of the letter which relate to the question of his marriage are as follows :—

'First of all in the matter of taking a wife, I reply that in respect of her whom you wished at first to give me I am quite content, and I thank God continually that I neither took her nor any other, and in this I have been wiser than you who wished to give her to me. I am sure that you will recognise now that if I had done as you wished I should not be in my present position, for I have now property in Rome of the value of three thousand gold ducats and an income of fifty gold scudi. Then his Holiness gives me a salary of three hundred gold ducats for superintending the fabric of S. Peter's, which will be continued as long as I live, and I am certain to earn money from others; and then I am paid for what work I do at my own valuation. And I have begun to paint another room for his Holiness which will bring me in twelve hundred gold ducats. So then, my dearest uncle, I do honour to you and to all my relations and to my native state. But for all that I have you always in my heart, and when I hear your name it is as though I heard that of my own father.'

Then, after reverting to the opening theme of the irregularity of the correspondence, he continues :—

'I have left off speaking about my marriage, but return to it to tell you that Santa Maria in Portico (Cardinal Bibbiena) wishes to give me one of his relatives, and with your leave and that of my uncle the priest I have promised to do what his Reverence desires. I cannot break my word; we are nearer than ever to bringing things to a conclusion, and soon I will tell you all about it. Have patience, for the matter is on the way to being settled well, and if it does not come off, then I will do as you wish. And know that if Francesco Buffa has offers for me I have some of my own also, for I can find a beautiful maiden here in Rome, and according to what I hear both she and her relatives bear very good reputations, and they are prepared to give a dowry of three thousand gold scudi invested in house property in Rome, and a hundred ducats here are worth more than two hundred in Urbino; of this be assured.'

As regards his uncle's views about his living in Rome he points out that he can never live anywhere else at any time, because of his having taken Bramante's place in the care of the fabric of S. Peter's, and adds with eloquence and warmth of feeling, ' But what place in the world can compare with Rome ? What enterprise is more worthy than this of S. Peter's, which is the first temple in the world ? It is the greatest building that has ever been seen, and it will cost more than a million in gold ; and know that the Pope has decided to spend annually sixty thousand ducats on the fabric, and that he thinks of nothing else.'

He adds that the Pope has appointed as his colleague in the care of the fabric, the aged Fra Giocondo, so that he may learn his secrets in architecture, and that his Holiness sends for them every day to discuss the works.

There is a characteristically confident touch in the

PERSONALITY

concluding paragraph of the letter in which he requests his uncle to go to the Duke and Duchess, to whom he sends his respectful greetings, and to tell them about him, 'for I know that they will be pleased to hear that one of their servants is doing them honour.'

Vasari attributes the delay in the negotiations for the marriage with the niece of Cardinal Bibbiena to the fact that Raphael had received an intimation that when the work upon which he was engaged in the Vatican was completed, the Pope intended to create him a Cardinal. The bestowal of such a dignity upon an artist would have been entirely without precedent. But so also was the princely retinue which attended him during his latter years at Rome. The letters show how confidently he would have worn the purple.

CHAPTER IV

PLACE IN ART

ALL art is the expression of the creative impulse. By the use of certain mediums the artist's conception becomes visualised, and is defined in terms of line, form and colour. Its primordial quality is originality. In the manner of its expression, however, a certain common factor may be discerned in work produced under similar conditions of time or place. Subtract, so far as may be, what this implies from the sum of artistic achievement, separating the individual from the mass; what remains is the ultimate vitalising factor of personality, which expresses itself with a dominance more or less sharply defined, according as the artist's primary purpose is such as to place him in the category of those who initiate, or those whose function it is to develop and to fulfil.

The singleness of influence of the first class, the debt being to nature, tends to create a certain superior homogeneity. Although in the second class nature is only one of many teachers, she is in a sense the teacher of all the rest, their knowledge having come by observation and practice. Leonardo is a type of the first. In following the record of his wanderings from Florence to Milan and back again to Florence and to Rome, there is little thought of what opportunities of studying the work of other artists he may have gained by migration. Wherever he might be he was following up principles to their issue by research, and his art is self-contained even from before the time when he left Verrocchio's studio. Raphael's name belongs no less naturally to the second category. His art is assimilative and receptive of influences to a degree unparalleled by any other of the greater masters of the Renaissance. His fame is in part due to this degree of receptivity, by virtue of which his art came to seem, as it were, the resultant of many forces. Like a river into which numberless streams have found their inevitable way, it gathers up into itself and expresses the aims and purposes of the artists of the preceding century and of his own more completely than can be claimed of any other single achievement.

Vasari tells how when Raphael died, in the plenitude of artistic power,—felix opportunitate mortis,—the unfinished picture of the *Transfiguration*, which the verdict of contemporary opinion acclaimed as his masterpiece, stood in the upper end of the hall, where he had worked upon it, when the body lay in state to be seen by the Roman crowd who came to look their last upon it before it was taken to the Pantheon for burial. The scene has a factor in common with one of very different circumstance, also described by Vasari—not without suspicion of legend—in which a great concourse paid homage to an artist's work in joy at its creation, so that the quarter of Florence became known as the Borgo Allegri because of the plaudits which marked the occasion of the display of Cimabue's 'Madonna.' The two scenes serve to typify the inception and close of the period of activity of the central tradition of Italian art. It was an art primarily of fresco and altarpiece,—an art of symbols fashioned at the bidding of the Church, as closely as ever were the creations of the Byzantine masters, in order to serve as the mirror of her teaching. By degrees the manner of the fashioning was guided and controlled by a closer perception of the forms and laws of nature and by the study of the art of antiquity; and finally, in what has been termed the High Renaissance, the knowledge thus gained was applied to the task of expressing and clothing in entirely natural forms the emotions of the human spirit and to satisfying the desire of the eyes, seeking thus in art to perpetuate the beauty of life.

All the greater names of record of the High Renaissance express in their works the different phases of this fuller freedom, Raphael with most emphasis in the *Galatea* and the work in portraiture of the Roman period.

Side by side with this wider utterance continued the central tradition of altarpiece and fresco as the mirror of teaching, and this tradition the work of Raphael fulfilled more comprehensively, and with a more complete admixture of spontaneity and ordered judgment, than are to be found in the work of any other painter. Upon a natural heritage of Umbrian simplicity, quietude, and feeling for beauty, were superimposed the elements of Florentine naturalism, with its new-found delight in form and precision of structure; and to these again, lest his art should be obsessed inordinately with science, came the freer life of Rome adding its gift of symmetry and a deeper perception of the mystery of colour.

Modern art, which may be said to have begun with Rembrandt and Velasquez, touches life at wider issues than the art of the Renaissance ever compassed. The latter artist, influenced in part, no doubt, by the spectacle of the works of Raphael's assistants in the Prado, there attributed to the master himself, openly professed his indifference to him as a painter. In proportion as his work was the perfected utterance of that central tradition of Italian art, it was the less a living influence when that tradition had ceased. By contrast with Correggio's idyllic visions of light and movement, achieved in solitude far from the greater art centres, or Michelangelo's sublime forms in the Sistine, both of which have a fellowship free of Time with some of the greatest of modern achievement, the work of Raphael, in its remoteness, its quietude, and purity of colour and line, seems as a garden sealed, and only those have won entrance who, like Ingres or David, have sought and found an ideal in the past. The living channels of art have passed it by.

Passavant, in a biography of which the value has been hardly if at all impaired by the research of three-quarters of a century, reveals the comparative instability of criticism by such a dictum as this :—'Raphael is now universally acknowledged to be the greatest genius of modern painting.'

As to which let us premise that there is no universal acknowledgment of anything in questions of art, and that, further, such pre-eminence as is here claimed would find practically no support in modern criticism. No work of Raphael's can be adjudged equal in sublimity of conception or sustained power of execution to the ceiling of the Sistine Chapel, and yet Raphael's achievement forms as great a rounded whole as does that of Michelangelo.

We turn rather to the old time catholicity of *The Courtier*, the more apposite in that the writer was the friend of Raphael.

'To know the true perfection,' says Castiglione, 'is in everything so hard a matter as to be almost impossible, and that by reason of the variety of judgments.'

But then, like a true critic, putting all these aside, he sees with his own eyes and thus defines the landmarks :

'Behold in painting Leonardo da Vinci, Mantegna, Raphael, Michelangelo, George of Castelfranco; they are all most excellent doers, yet are they in working unlike, but in any of them a man would not judge that there wanted aught in his kind of trade, for every one is known to be of most perfection after his manner.'

Add Correggio and Titian, and although there are Alps on Alps still remaining, the summits are named.

RAPHAEL SANTI
TWENTY PLATES IN COLOUR, EXECUTED
UNDER THE SUPERVISION OF THE
MEDICI SOCIETY

I

THE VISION OF A KNIGHT

NATIONAL GALLERY

A YOUNG knight, clad in armour, lying asleep at the foot of a laurel; two figures seen approaching, the one grave, demure of aspect, clad very simply in violet robe, looking down at him and holding out in one hand a sword, in the other a book; the other, softer and more alluring, with clinging, diaphanous robe, adorned with strings of coral and radiant with sunlight, holding out a sprig of myrtle: the laurel stem parting the background in two, with result that behind the one figure is a vision of fortress and hill with road winding steeply upward, and on the summit a gaunt bare rock and a building crowned with a tall spire; behind the other is seen a watered valley meandering among gently sloping hills, and along it are towers and palaces and a bridge with a watch-tower, all steeped in sunshine; the manner of the whole timid and tentative, the types showing some rusticity, but joyous with an indescribable air of freshness and youth. Is it all a transcript from the book of pure romance? Or must the critic labour to interpret and identify in fields of mythology, hagiology, and the like? The sum of Gibeonitish endeavours is ever growing. It passed formerly under the title 'The Dream of S. George.' In just such another small panel as this Raphael depicted the Cappadocian in combat, but the sleeping knight has none of the attributes of sainthood. More recently it has been adjudged to be an illustration of the old fable of the choice of Hercules, told perhaps most fully in Xenophon's *Memorabilia* as remembered from the lips of the teacher Prodicus. But Hercules was not sleeping when the two women appeared, he was sitting debating within himself; and the figure asleep beneath the laurel has none of the hero's conventional properties, lion's skin or club, or sovereign strength of limb; his delicately fashioned features convey no suggestion of one whose character is a personification of ideal strength and energy.

The resemblance which undoubtedly exists between the features of the sleeping knight and those of the painter himself, as shown in the self-portrait in the Pitti Palace—seen in the arch of the eyebrows, the pure oval of the face, the aquiline nose with nostrils very slightly dilated, the mobile, quivering mouth, the look of delicacy and innate refinement—suggests a more intimate meaning to the allegory. In the words of a recent biographer, M. Gillet, 'the myth of the crossways, which every man comes to as he goes on his pathway, and which Greece expressed by the fable of the choice of Hercules, is as old as the world itself.' The choice is as old as human nature, and Raphael was of the number who make it at the outset. The germ of the conception here in-

The Vision of a Knight
National Gallery

THE VISION OF A KNIGHT

terpreted may perhaps be derived from a woodcut of the 'Strife of Virtue with Pleasure' in Sebastian Brandt's *Ship of Fools*, which, as M. de Maulde la Clavière has shown in an article in the *Gazette des Beaux Arts* (Jan. 1897), presents a somewhat close parallel, although in the woodcut the note of allegory is much more dominant. Immediately behind the figure of the sleeping knight are two small hills up which paths lead, the one easy, the other steep and stony, and at the summits stand the two figures: the one bare and meretricious, behind whom crouches a skeleton, the other wearing the dress of a nun. The *Stultifera navis* made its first appearance in 1494, and numerous editions and translations bear witness to the immediate popularity of the work. A copy of it may well have found its way to the Library at Urbino, for the Duke Federigo's rigorous preference for manuscripts over printed books was not maintained by his successor. There Raphael may have seen it, and, attracted by the subject of the woodcut, may have set himself to interpret its meaning in more melodious line. Whether he knew Brandt's work or no, the occasion for the panel is to be found in his life at Urbino. Crowe and Cavalcaselle, who regard it as a product of a visit paid by Raphael to Urbino in 1504, which 'combines Peruginesque style with a more delicate strain of Raphaelesque thought,' connect it with the discourses given, according to Castiglione, in the salon of the Duchess 'for the conduct of true lovers, polished courtiers, and accomplished soldiers.' Far more credible

RAPHAEL SANTI

is the hypothesis of Morelli that it was one of Raphael's earliest works, executed at Urbino before he went to Perugia. The traces of the Peruginesque are remarkably few. The dominant influence is ruder and simpler. The chromatic suggestion is of the warm sober hues of the Ferrarese, and in colouring, landscape, and such details as treatment of drapery and hands, the picture forms an important link in the chain of evidence by which Morelli seeks to prove the existence of a pre-Peruginesque period in his art, and the fact of his pupilage under Timoteo Viti on the return of the latter to Urbino in 1495 after a period of five years in the studio of Francia in Bologna. Giovanni Santi having died in the previous year, and Raphael having remained in association with his assistant Evangelista di Pian di Meleto.

The picture is one of several which may be assigned tentatively to the year 1499, at the close of which Raphael, then in his eighteenth year, left Urbino for Perugia. All small and carefully finished, with an almost miniature-like precision, they seem to be the work of one who had often pored over the pages of missals and illuminated manuscripts in the library at Urbino, where all the arts found quiet anchorage under the gentle rule of Guidobaldo and his duchess Elisabetta Gonzaga. The panel, seven inches square, dainty as a cameo, in colouring subdued but vibrant with harmony, breathes an unforgettable air of youth and naïveté. It seems as it were a very personification of maiden thought. Rarely have the first beginnings of artistic genius found ex-

THE VISION OF A KNIGHT

pression so idyllic, or a theme so entirely personal and unfettered by tradition.

The picture was in the Borghese Collection in about the middle of the seventeenth century, having been removed to Rome from Urbino according to Morelli, together with the 'Three Graces' and the portrait of Perugino now in the Borghese. It was acquired from the Borghese by W. Young Ottley at the end of the eighteenth century, and, after passing through the Lawrence, Sykes, and Egerton Collections, it was bought for the National Gallery in 1847. There also, immediately below it, hangs the original cartoon for the picture—a drawing with the pen in sepia pricked for transfer to the panel.

II

THE MADONNA CONESTABILE

HERMITAGE GALLERY, PETROGRAD

RAPHAEL produced certain masterpieces in portraiture, and his work in the Vatican renders evident his supreme genius as a space composer, yet his name is associated primarily with the representation in art of the Virgin and Child. Giotto had vindicated the freedom of art to express the essential humanity of the relation; it lay with Raphael, heir to the art of Piero de' Franceschi, inheritor of the traditions of the pietistic art of Umbria, to re-establish in its fulness, in terms of a scientific precision acquired by contact with the Florentines, its deep, all-pervading mystery, by virtue of which he is the crowning figure in the development of the central tradition of Italian art.

His various Madonna pictures may be considered as marking the stages in the realisation of this ideal, with the reservation that in any attempt to define the chronological sequence of works, of which the only evidence consists of the somewhat intangible data of stylistic indications, conclusions must of necessity be of a somewhat tentative nature. A certain chameleon-like

THE MADONNA CONESTABILE

quality perceptible in the art of Raphael during its earlier stages enhances the difficulty of the problem in no slight degree, and the evidence of drawings is not a sure ground for inference in questions of authenticity, owing to the practice—a fairly common one—of the assistant executing a commission from a drawing by the master. The similar use of a pupil's drawing by a master, although naturally less frequent, is not unknown.

The earliest Madonnas, small cabinet pictures carefully finished, which, like the early figure panels, serve to link his art to that of the miniaturist, were all originally private commissions; their existence remained unknown to historian and biographer until in course of time they passed by purchase into public collections. Four of these seem to have a natural priority, the *Madonna Conestabile della Staffa*, also known as the *Madonna del Libro*, at the Hermitage Gallery, and the *Madonna and Child with S. Jerome and S. Francis*, and the *Diotalevi* and *Solly Madonnas* all at Berlin. The three last undoubtedly date from the period at which Raphael had become acquainted with the work of Perugino and Pinturicchio, and Morelli who considers them all derived from drawings by the latter, assigns them to the period of Raphael's close association with Pinturicchio, which followed immediately on the departure of Perugino from Perugia to Florence in the autumn of 1502, his absence continuing during the best part of the two following years. In the case of the *Diotalevi Madonna*, so called after the family who were originally its possessors, the dominance of Pinturicchio's influence is incontestable, but as regards the *Madonna and Child with S. Jerome and S. Francis* and the *Solly Madonna* it is open to question, the influence of Perugino being by no means negligible, and the drawing which Raphael used for the first being assigned to Perugino by Passavant, and Crowe and Cavalcaselle.

Certain drawings ascribed by general consent to Raphael serve as intermediate terms to link together the *Madonna Conestabile*, the *Madonna and Child with S. Jerome and S. Francis* and the *Solly Madonna*. The first of these, a pen drawing in the University Galleries at Oxford, representing a very youthful Madonna with the Child—the latter being repeated with delicious freedom of curving line on the reverse of the sheet—is possibly the earliest extant specimen of Raphael's numerous attempts to represent the subject. Fashioned apparently throughout with light quick strokes, it seems endowed with the transparent simplicity and freshness of first conception. We may note the Timotesque breadth of hand here as in the *Vision of a Knight*, the architectural features of the background possessing a general similarity to those of the *Vision* and of the Berlin *Madonna with S. Jerome and S. Francis*. The lower half of the body of the child is almost exactly the same as in the latter picture, but in the figure of the Virgin the treatment of the dress and the stately carriage of the head the analogy lies rather with the *Madonna Conestabile*.

The Madonna Conestabile
Hermitage Gallery, Petrograd

THE MADONNA CONESTABILE

Other studies more closely connected with this picture are a drawing with the pen at Berlin, and a charcoal drawing in the Albertina, which Morelli styles a modified imitation of that at Berlin. The Berlin drawing he assigns on stylistic grounds to Perugino, whereas Crowe and Cavalcaselle and M. Somof, the Director of the Hermitage, in his 'Catalogue Raisonné,' regard it as an authentic work by Raphael; all critics, however, are agreed in considering it to be the sketch which Raphael made use of when he was at work on the picture. These two drawings—that at Berlin and that in the Albertina—show a pomegranate in the hand of the Virgin which the Child is touching. In the picture the Virgin is holding a book; but that this was an afterthought was rendered evident soon after its acquisition by the Hermitage, when the picture was transferred from panel to canvas because a crack had appeared across its surface, and it was found that in the first state of the picture the Virgin had held a pomegranate and not a book. The book, which also appears in the sketch in the Albertina lying open on the bench with the Virgin's other hand resting on it, is held in the right hand in place of the pomegranate in the pen drawing of a Virgin and Child in the Louvre, which, from the treatment of the drapery and general stylistic indications Morelli assigns to Pinturicchio, but which was used by Raphael for the *Solly Madonna* with somewhat more freedom in divergence of detail than he allowed himself in the case of the Berlin sketch and the *Madonna*

Conestabile. 'The close relationship of the Louvre sketch ... with the *Madonna Conestabile* and other varieties in which the book is a leading feature shows,' according to Crowe and Cavalcaselle, 'how long and how constantly Raphael meditated over themes, the originals of which he had found in the studio of Perugino.'

The evidence presented by these drawings, although not very definite, seems to point to a priority in date of composition of the Hermitage picture, and this is not in any degree impugned by the picture itself. The simplicity of conception causes it to have a position among Raphael's Madonna pictures analogous to that which the Oxford drawing has among the studies. As a consequence of this simplicity there is a marked absence of Peruginesque mannerisms. The picture seems to date from a transition stage when no one influence was dominant, and Raphael was relatively for a time his own master. The question then arises whether it was painted when he was only beginning to pass under Perugino's influence or when he was endeavouring to emancipate himself from it; in other words, Was the picture painted before or after the *Mond Crucifixion*? Morelli favours the latter alternative and assigns it to 1503, the year of Perugino's absence from Perugia, when, as he says, 'Raphael, left to himself, seems to have endeavoured gradually, under the guidance of his own great genius, to emancipate himself from the Perugian manner.' Crowe and Cavalcaselle and von Seidlitz assign it to a somewhat later date in

THE MADONNA CONESTABILE

the Perugian period, and Venturi places it later still at a date subsequent to the first visit to Florence. Müntz, Gronau and others, on the other hand, ascribe it to the very beginning of the Perugian period, Gronau estimating the date as between 1500 and 1502, and this conclusion seems to be most in accordance with the evidence presented by the picture. In spite of the undoubted traces of Peruginesque form and feeling the prevailing mood is Umbrian. Figure and landscape possess that romantic simplicity which Raphael caught in part from Timoteo Viti, but which his own natural instinct strove to intensify.

The head of the Virgin may be compared with the similarly inclined head of the figure which personifies Pleasure in the *Vision of a Knight*. The advance in strength and firmness of modelling, and in depth of chiaroscuro, is significant, but it is not in excess of what Raphael might conceivably accomplish in one or two years. When he was passing away from the domination of Perugino's influence a few mannerisms remained, but at the date at which he executed the *Madonna Conestabile* he had gained nothing but good from his association with the elder painter.

Müntz says that the snow-capped mountains in the background of the picture were painted from nature in the neighbourhood of Perugia, and suggests that the broad expanse of water upon which fishermen are seen rowing a boat may be a reminiscence of a visit to Lake Trasimene.

RAPHAEL SANTI

After belonging originally to Alfano di Diamante of Perugia the picture remained in the possession of the Alfani family, who, at the commencement of the eighteenth century, took the title of Counts della Staffa. In 1789 it passed into the ownership of the Counts Conestabili, from whom it was acquired in 1870 by the Czar Alexander II. He presented it to the Czarina, and it hung in the Winter Palace until her death, which occurred in 1880, when, under the terms of her will, it passed into the Hermitage Collection.

III

THE CRUCIFIXION

MOND COLLECTION, LONDON

THE picture was a commission, executed probably in 1502-3, for the chapel of the Gavari family in S. Domenico at Città di Castello, where it remained for over three hundred years. It is the second in order of composition of the three altarpieces which Raphael made for patrons at Città di Castello after he had entered Perugino's studio at Perugia, during the period when Perugino was absent while engaged upon commissions. The first was that of the *Coronation of S. Nicolo da Tolentino* in which his father's assistant Evangelista di Pian di Meleto was associated with him. The *Crucifixion* probably followed it immediately. Executed in Perugino's studio in the presence of many examples of the master's work, it marks the complete although temporary divergence from the influences of the art of Timoteo Viti and Giovanni Santi.

The subject of the composition is not the Crucifixion considered as an historical event—in that case there would be an anachronism in the introduction of the figure of S. Jerome. Dr Richter, whose notice of the picture in his work on the Mond Collection is by far the most complete, has pointed out that the altarpiece represents the conception of the body and blood of Christ, offered first on the Cross and then, mystically, in the Eucharist, adored by the faithful in the persons of the Magdalen and S. Jerome; thus illustrating the words of the Office for Good Friday in the Roman Missal:—

> 'Crucem tuam adoramus, Domine ... ecce enim propter lignum venit gaudium in universo mundo.'

The Virgin and S. John, who stand a little distance apart from the foot of the Cross and do not share the emotion of the two kneeling saints, are to be looked upon as completing the traditional representation of the Crucifixion.

At the foot of the Cross is the painter's signature in Roman letters set in gold—

> RAPHAEL
> VRBIN
> AS
> P

'and if his name was not written there,' says Vasari, 'no one would believe it to be the work of Raphael, but rather of Pietro Perugino.'

The arraignment of Vasari is one of the amenities of modern art criticism, and this statement has not passed unchallenged. That it contains a fundamental element of truth would seem to follow from the fact that the

The Crucifixion
Mond Collection, London

THE CRUCIFIXION

altarpiece represents the stage in the evolution of the art of Raphael in which he is most completely dominated by that of Perugino.

On entering the latter's studio, which he did in 1499 or 1500, in the capacity rather of an assistant than a pupil, his work had been to 'lay in' large altarpieces in fulfilment of Perugino's many commissions, to execute the subsidiary parts of these, and in the case of lesser commissions to proceed to execute them from Perugino's drawings. This in fact also happened with the *Crucifixion*, although Raphael claimed the authorship by his signature. Morelli has pointed out a sequence of works by Perugino, from which the parts of it are directly derived. The figure of Christ is taken from a drawing by Perugino of about 1470 to 1475 for his altarpiece in the Calza at Florence; the two angels are derived from the fresco in the Cambio at Perugia, and also occur in Perugino's 'Resurrection' in the Vatican; the S. John is taken from the drawing which Perugino used for his 'Deposition,' now in the Pitti; the other figures, the Virgin, S. Mary Magdalen and S. Jerome, according to the same critic, are derived more or less closely from drawings used by Perugino either for the great fresco in S. Maria Maddalena dei Pazzi in Florence, or for the 'Crucifixion' in the Florentine Academy.

The substantial truth of these attributions is obvious on a comparison of photographs. Where Raphael's personality finds expression is in a certain refining and ennobling of types. His borrowings as yet trammel him no whit the more than do Shakespeare's. All the Peruginesque he assimilated apparently without effort. The result was different when he came within the orbits of Leonardo and Michelangelo. At the time of the *Crucifixion* his art was already in essence the perfection of the distinctively Umbrian tenets. Already he had shown himself as space composer and in dignity and grace of line the ultimate heir of the art of Piero de' Franceschi. Modelling his figures on those of Perugino, his superiority in sincerity, power of expression and arrangement, is manifest by a comparison with the 'Crucifixion' which the latter painted in the autumn of 1510 for the Chigi altar in S. Agostino at Siena, in which the multiplicity of saints and cherubs set against a row of quivering aspens distracts and disturbs.

The picture remained in S. Domenico from 1503, the date being fixed by an inscription on the altar, until 1818, when it was purchased by Cardinal Fesch. At the sale of the Cardinal's pictures in 1845 it was bought by the Prince of Canino. Two years afterwards it passed into the possession of Lord Ward, afterwards the first Earl of Dudley, in whose collection it remained until the year 1892, when it was acquired by the late Dr. Mond.

A difference of nearly ten inches between the height of the picture and that of the frame tends directly to corroborate a tradition that the picture once had a predella, which is said to have been given as a present to a cardinal. Two small predella-like pictures, which belong apparently to the same period of Raphael's activity

THE CRUCIFIXION

—the *S. Jerome Punishing the Heretic Sabinianus* in Sir Frederick Cook's Collection at Richmond, and *S. Cyril Resuscitating Three Dead Men* in the Gallery at Lisbon—may be regarded as having probably once formed part of it. The identification is strengthened in the one case by the fact that the saint is one of those who are represented in the altarpiece.

IV.

THE MARRIAGE OF THE VIRGIN (LO SPOSALIZIO)

BRERA GALLERY, MILAN

THE *Sposalizio* was the latest of three commissions executed by Raphael for patrons at Città di Castello during the absence from Perugia of Perugino owing to his being occupied with work in Florence. Vasari's mention of the circumstances immediately follows his notice of the *Crucifixion*, which, he says 'but for the signature would be supposed by every one to be a work by Pietro Perugino.' 'In S. Francesco also in the same city,' he continues, 'he represented in a small picture the marriage of Our Lady, wherein may be distinctly seen the progress of excellence of Raphael's style, which becomes much more subtle and refined, and surpasses the manner of Pietro. In this work there is a temple drawn in perspective with such evident care that it is marvellous to behold the difficulty of the problems which he has there set himself to solve.'

Between the two commissions here noticed the *Coronation of the Virgin*, and perhaps one or two Madonna pictures, intervened. The nearness of the two in date of composition—the *Sposalizio* bearing the

THE MARRIAGE OF THE VIRGIN

date 1504 and the *Crucifixion* being in all probability a year earlier—illustrates the rapidity of the growth of power in the art of Raphael. The substantial accuracy of Vasari's testimony as to each is incontestable. In the former Raphael is satisfied 'to play the sedulous ape,' although the result is in some respects superior to his models. In the *Sposalizio* he is using formulas which he is conscious that he has outgrown.

The composition of the picture is entirely symmetrical. Formalism would seem inevitable in the group in the foreground, where on either side of the high priest the Virgin and S. Joseph have each a train of five followers. He has tried to veil this by the rhythmical balance of the figures and the naturalness of the action; most successfully in the case of the Virgin and her women. Four of the latter are purely Peruginesque types, but the majestic figure in the foreground has something of Timoteo Viti's solidity, and the graceful carriage and simplicity of the figure of the Virgin cause it almost to seem a prototype of the Madonnas of the Florentine period. S. Joseph and the suitor bending down in sharp foreshortening and breaking his rod across his knee are both taken from Perugino's predella at Fano, and much improved in the taking, as was Raphael's manner, but the attitude of S. Joseph is inherently artificial; his feet are crossed like those of a dancing master; the arm which is stretched out to place the ring on the Virgin's finger seems too long for the body, as is also that of the Virgin which meets it.

RAPHAEL SANTI

This is perhaps an unforeseen result of the attempt to heighten the significance of the central group by increasing the distance between the characters. The somewhat nonchalant-looking youthful suitor on the right, who is breaking his rod by bending it in his hands, is derived presumably from the same model as the figure immediately on the left of the Virgin, and each would seem to be based on a drawing by Perugino.

The symmetry of arrangement extends to the middle distance, to the dispositions of the groups and the patterns of the pavement, to the open colonnades of the temple and the sloping contours of the distant hills which bound the horizon on either side. It lacks therefore the ultimate touches of freedom of conception. The architectural exactitude of line of the temple, which seems to reveal a memory of Piero de' Franceschi's architectural study preserved in the ducal palace at Urbino, imposes its own rule of symmetry upon the figures in the piazza. But what rifts of sky there are through door and open colonnades! What blue depth in the Umbrian distance! What a deep green in the summer foliage! The whole scene is steeped in clear sunlight, in which the soft harmony of colours is rendered more impressive. It is all Umbrian in spirit in that it is entirely contemplative. The characters are rapt in reverie. The bent rods of the suitors do not break, and it is no effort for the holders thus to stand.

Except for the inversion in the order of the characters, the men being shown on the right of the high priest

The Marriage of the Virgin (Lo Sposalizio)
Brera Gallery, Milan

THE MARRIAGE OF THE VIRGIN

and the women on the left, the scheme of distribution and general composition of the picture is practically identical with that of the *Sposalizio* in the Museum at Caen, which was in the chapel of S. Joseph in the Cathedral at Perugia until Napoleon ordered the removal of art treasures from Italy. It was attributed by Vasari to Perugino, and has been traditionally regarded as the prototype of Raphael's picture, to which it is far inferior in artistic qualities, as would naturally be inferred from Vasari's statement as to Raphael's picture. Mr. Berenson would reverse the traditional order of precedence of the two pictures, and regards that at Caen as a free copy of Raphael's picture, made about four years after it by Lo Spagna. Signor Venturi is entirely in accord with Mr. Berenson in rejecting the traditional ascription to Perugino, and is convinced, on general stylistic considerations, that the Caen picture is a copy of Raphael's by another of Perugino's pupils, Andrea d'Assisi.

The logic of documentary facts, as marshalled by the latest historian of the art of Perugia, Herr Bombe, goes far to re-establish the verdict of tradition as against the conclusions of adventurous connoisseurship.

He shows that the commission for the picture in the chapel of S. Joseph was given to Perugino in 1499. Various delays occurred, owing probably to Perugino's work in the Cambio. That the picture was not completed in 1503 is proved by the will of a merchant of the city dated Dec. 26, 1503, who left a legacy to be paid on the completion of the picture to Perugino, ' or to whatever other master should finish it.' But this also shows that it had already been commenced, and consequently it cannot be looked upon as a copy of Raphael's picture, which bears the date 1504, but is the earlier version from which Raphael's composition is derived, although the two may have been worked upon at the same time.

The evidence of tradition in favour of Perugino's authorship is somewhat strengthened by the *provenance* of the picture. Whatever his practice may have been as regards distant commissions, it is unlikely that Perugino would have entrusted to a pupil the execution of an altarpiece for the Cathedral of Perugia.

The *Sposalizio*, which bears on the moulding of the central arch of the temple the dated signature, RAPHAEL VRBINAS, MDIIII, was, according to a recently discovered document, a commission from a certain Filippo degli Albezzini. It remained over an altar in S. Francesco in Città di Castello until the year 1798, when it was surrendered on the demand of a General Giuseppi Lecchi, who was at the time in command of a French Brigade stationed in the town. Lecchi, three years afterwards, sold his booty to Giacomo Sannazaro of Milan, who died three years later, and by his will bequeathed it to the Hospital of Milan. It was bought, for 53,000 francs, from the Hospital for the State in the year 1806, and placed in the Gallery of the Brera, where it has since remained, although when the French army entered Milan in 1859 there was a proposal that the picture should be offered as a gift to France.

V

THE MADONNA DEL GRAN DUCA

PITTI GALLERY, FLORENCE

BY the common consent of critics the *Madonna del Gran Duca* is looked upon as one of the earliest of the works undertaken by Raphael after his visit to Florence. The unanimity is the more striking because it is unsupported by documentary evidence, the exact occasion and circumstances of the origin of the picture being unknown. Stylistic considerations give it a certain priority among the various representations of the Madonna and Child in which Florentine influences are superimposed upon those of Umbria and Perugia. By contrast with the creations of his Umbrian period—studies of emotion, pietistic, ecstatic or contemplative—the intermingling of Florentine influences is as the breath of a larger air. No sooner did he set foot in Florence—the letter of October 1st, 1504, in which Giovanna della Rovere commended him to the Gonfaloniere of Florence, Pier Soderini, supplying the date approximately—than he was fired by the examples of art which he saw there to attempt to represent the beauty of reality; this in the Madonna and Child found expression in the portrayal of the natural relationship. Consequently, as has been well said, the charm of his Florentine Madonnas consists in the fact that they are simply human. The simplicity of structure of the *Madonna del Gran Duca*— a half-length with the principal figure erect, the Child held seated but upright with vertical functional lines—causes it to seem a natural starting-point. Gradually he was to introduce greater freedom and more vigorous movement, and to diversify the action by the use of additional figures; but in the inception of purpose simplicity is rendered more emphatic by the omission of all accessories. The figures stand out against a uniform dull background as though in relief. The Virgin's robe and mantle, conceived on Peruginesque lines, offer simple colour contrasts of red, blue and green. The charm of the picture consists in the absolute naturalness of the relation of the Madonna to the Child. Her face is soft and virginal. The perfect oval of the head, the curve of lips gathered in daintily have some suggestion of Timoteo Viti to whose more luminous flesh tints the work shows a greater resemblance, according to Morelli, than to those of darker tone of Perugino. But Peruginesque influence is not confined to the drapery; a certain dreaming abstraction, an air as of reverie on the face of the Madonna may be attributed directly to it, and a certain chubbiness in the figure of the Child.

In a drawing in the Uffizi (No. 4)—apparently the first conception of the composition—the Virgin has a more pronounced expression of Peruginesque melancholy,

The Madonna del Gran Duca
Pitti Gallery, Florence

THE MADONNA DEL GRAN DUCA

yet, as Crowe and Cavalcaselle remark, 'even the sketches which precede and accompany the picture have felt the breath of the Florentine air.'

On the two sides of another sheet in the Uffizi the same model appears in sketches for this picture and for the *Madonna di Casa Tempi*; in the latter picture Raphael, while preserving the same simplicity of composition, succeeded in obtaining a more entirely natural attitude for the Child, in which the new exuberance of life found more spontaneous expression.

The firm, true modelling of the flesh and the softly rounded limbs of the Child in the *Gran Duca*—far in advance of any of the pre-Florentine work in virility and scientific precision—reveals the study of Donatello, and this is still more pronounced in the *Madonna di Casa Tempi*, which, on the evidence of the abovementioned sheet of studies, may be considered as having immediately succeeded it. Vasari tells of Raphael having been stimulated to visit Florence by reports of the excellence of the great cartoons which Leonardo and Michelangelo had executed for the Palazzo della Signoria, but this can only have reference to his second visit in 1506 since at the time of the first visit the cartoons were not completed. The evidence presented by the two Madonna pictures points to a close study of the work of Donatello having preceded that of both his two great contemporaries. The work offered a far greater similarity of subject. In the composition of the *S. George* in the Hermitage, executed certainly within twelve months of these pictures, Raphael not only assimilated but frankly borrowed a leading motive from the sculptor. In the *Madonna del Gran Duca* and *di Casa Tempi* this influence is visible in its inception. Together with the study of Masaccio's work in the Brancacci Chapel of the Carmine it formed an underlying basis of unity in the work of his Florentine period.

Carotti has suggested that the *Madonna del Gran Duca* was one of two small Madonna pictures which, according to Vasari, Raphael painted at Urbino for the Duke Guidobaldo during a visit he paid to that city from Florence on family affairs, probably in the autumn of 1506. The evidence seems, however, to point to an earlier date of composition.

The picture is said to have once belonged to Carlo Dolci. Its subsequent history is unknown until the close of the eighteenth century, when it passed from the possession of a poor widow in Florence to a bookseller for twelve scudi, the equivalent of about fifty shillings. In the year 1799 it was acquired for three hundred sequins (£140) by Puccini, the Director of the Florence Gallery, on behalf of the Grand Duke of Tuscany, Ferdinand III. The Grand Duke, after whom the picture has received its name, displayed an extraordinary affection for it, and caused it to be taken about with him wherever he went; it accompanied him into exile. Since 1859 it has been in the Pitti Gallery.

VI

THE PORTRAIT OF ANGELO DONI

PITTI GALLERY, FLORENCE

IT was to a Florentine merchant, Angelo Doni—that frugal Mæcenas, who, according to Vasari, was unwilling to spend his money on anything except paintings and sculpture, and wished to acquire these as cheaply as possible,—who possessed pictures by Fra Bartolommeo and Michelangelo, and whose attempt to beat down the latter in the price he asked for the *tondo* of the Holy Family, now in the Tribuna of the Uffizi, proved singularly expensive, that Raphael owed the opportunity of his earliest commission as a painter of portraits.

His likenesses of Angelo and his wife Maddalena Strozzi were among the earliest of the works executed after his arrival in Florence. Their technique displays the working of the newer influences superimposed upon the Perugian training. Portraiture was the branch of art in which he matured latest; there is in the Doni portraits little to suggest the full rich harmonies of colour and the subtle blending of tones which characterise the portrait of

Baldassare Castiglione and the *La Velata*. Along with evident care of the minutest description there is a certain timidity in their execution as compared with the Madonna pictures of the period. The works have been characterised as superficial, as showing him, that is, as preoccupied solely with the material likeness. It would seem, however, that the *Angelo Doni*—the later probably of the two—in which the sobriety of method of Ghirlandaio has proved more attainable, supervening upon the more subtly conceived harmonies of Leonardo, visualises with some considerable precision the personality of the sitter as defined in the pages of Vasari.

It presents the type of the prosperous merchant. There is no apparent evidence of wealth, but such alertness as must surely obtain it. The keen, piercing eyes, the spare face, high cheek-bones, the firm mouth and thin lips, the aquiline nose, convey a hawk-like look, half of intelligence, half of avarice. The colour scheme is simple and effective. Black berretto, black robe with flowing red sleeves, present a vivid contrast. There is some suggestion in the figure of the warmth of Venetian work.

The portrait of *Maddalena Doni* is by contrast somewhat expressionless. The difference was no doubt in part due to the sitter's personality, which over-rode the painter's initial purpose. The type is that of the placid haus-frau, homely and burgher-like. She had been married at the age of fifteen, and being a daughter of the great Strozzi house of bankers, had brought with her a substantial dowry, and freed by her marriage from all un-

The Portrait of Angelo Doni
Pitti Gallery, Florence

certainty as to her future, had already, in the two years which intervened between her marriage and the time when the portrait was painted, acquired something of a matron-like air, although only in her eighteenth year.

Raphael, who, so soon as he reached Florence, set himself with eagerness to apprehend the rules and precepts of painting enunciated by Leonardo, listening there to his discourses on art theory, and studying zealously the application of them which the master had given in the 'Mona Lisa,' found himself in a position, in the opportunity afforded by the Doni commissions, to attempt to follow out the same principles.

At a later period of his activity he paid the same homage to Michelangelo. In both cases the attempt must be adjudged to have been made in vain, inasmuch as he lost temporarily the sincerity of personal utterance without gaining any equivalent measure of the subtilty, intensity, and depth of feeling of his exemplars. Two drawings at the Louvre and in the Wicar Museum at Lille reveal how fully he was absorbed by his search after Leonardesque expression. In the latter, a study of a woman drawn in silver point, in exactly the position of the 'Mona Lisa,' and with almost the same functional lines, something of the smile which for centuries has baffled the critic's powers of description is caught playing on the lips.

In the pen drawing in the Louvre, in all photographs of which the shadows are too dark, losing thereby some delicate nuance of expression in the large dreamy eyes and the passion of the indrawn curve of the mouth, we find a sketch for the *Maddalena Doni* so obviously inspired by the 'Mona Lisa' as to be in effect a free rendering of it, with contour lines firmer, with suggestion of youth, and some added freedom of hair, with headdress and shadows and the placing of arms and hands studied and followed with utmost fidelity.

The comparison of Raphael's picture with this sketch reveals how a part of this domination disappeared beneath the accumulated logic of facts. It was a likeness which he was commissioned to execute. By contrast, alike with the drawing and its prototype, the dress is much richer both in material and workmanship. The colours make up in variety what they lack in depth. In the sketch a plain bodice encloses the muslin pleats of a high dress. In the picture this has disappeared, and a background has been made for the display of the family jewels by the unveiling of an ample bosom. The fingers are adorned with rings, and the position of the hands is altered so that they are less in shadow. The lines of the figure are somewhat coarsened. Raphael has abandoned, reluctantly no doubt, the 'Mona Lisa' *motif*, and having done so he has set himself to paint with absolute fidelity what he saw before him, carrying out as far as practicable Leonardo's precepts, following him in the incidence of his lights and shadows, and his sense of movement as shown in the treatment of the hair, but not attempting anything of his depth of modelling or subtlety of expression. The result is a remarkable piece of realism which presents a purely

THE MADONNA OF THE MEADOW

follow the precept which reigned in art circles on the high authority of Fra Bartolommeo and Leonardo, whereby the head of the Madonna served as the apex of a pyramid or triangle, the sides of which were coterminous with the contour lines of the composition. The difficulty of the problem of how, within these limits, to attain the utmost freedom of natural movement supplies a sufficient reason why the number of preliminary sketches for the earlier compositions in this form are very numerous. Three pages of studies in the Albertina, first thoughts apparently for the *Madonna of the Meadow*, but some connected almost as closely with the *Madonna with the Goldfinch*, show him trying, first by one motive then by another, to combine the figures in an entirely natural relation. The sketches are slight and rapid, after Leonardo's precept, 'with details not too finished.' They aim merely at catching an attitude, a turn of head, or outstretched hand.

The final arrangement is shown in a drawing shaded with sepia in the University Galleries at Oxford (No. 33).

In Sir J. C. Robinson's *Critical Account of the Oxford Drawings* a certain difference of type and expression is noted as existing between the head of the Virgin in this drawing and that in the picture of the *Madonna of the Meadow*, the first 'based in some measure on the creations of Giovanni Santi and Perugino,' whereas the second 'approximates to the more mannered ideal of Leonardo.' The difference suggests that some period of time may perhaps have elapsed between the dates of composition of the drawing and the picture. The latter bears a date in Roman numerals in the centre of the embroidered hem at the top of the Virgin's robe. There is, however, a difference of opinion among Raphael's biographers as to whether or no the I which is separated from V by two circles, one within the other, should be considered as part of the date, and whether consequently it should be read as 1505 or 1506.

Stylistic considerations would suffice to place the date of composition near the commencement of the period of Raphael's residence in Florence. Although the arrangement, the treatment of the herbage, the type and figure of the Virgin, and the suffusion of light in the background are abundant proof of his study of the works and precepts of Leonardo da Vinci, the presence of Perugian influence is very perceptible in the general tone of the colour and in the composition of the landscape, with just such features as are found in certain of his earlier pictures; and in the attitude of the two children, the one kneeling to present a cross of reed, the other leaning forward to receive it, there is a certain Umbrian quietude altogether different from the action in the *Madonna with the Goldfinch*, where the S. John, who has just run up to show the bird, has a vitality entirely Florentine.

Morelli seeks to account for the temporary revival of old Perugian impressions in the *Madonna of the Meadow* by the suggestion that it was painted during the period of Raphael's visit to Perugia from Florence. He went there in the summer of 1505, and remained for the greater part of a year, being occupied with the frescoes

THE MADONNA OF THE MEADOW

at S. Severo and two large altarpieces. The proofs of the Florentine origin of the picture seem, however, circumstantial.

Vasari, in telling of the friendships which Raphael formed soon after arriving in Florence with painters and others, says that he was much esteemed in the city, but above all by Taddeo Taddei, who, being a great admirer of all men of distinguished talent, desired to have him constantly in his house and at his table.

A corroboration of Vasari's testimony, in so far as it relates to the character of Taddeo Taddei, is to be found in the fact that the latter was on terms of friendly intimacy with Cardinal Bembo, as is seen from the Cardinal's letters to him.

Raphael, who, according to Vasari, was kindliness itself, not being willing to be surpassed in generosity, painted for Taddeo two pictures 'wherein there are traces of his first manner derived from Pietro (Perugino) and of that other much better one which he afterwards acquired by study.' The pictures at the time at which Vasari wrote were still in the house of the heirs of the said Taddeo.

The account of the blending of the earlier and later manner is entirely applicable to the *Madonna of the Meadow*, but the positive evidence of identification is derived from Baldinucci, who in his *Notizie*, etc., of which the first edition appeared in 1681, says, referring to Vasari's statement, that one of the pictures was no longer visible at the house of the Taddei, and the other,

RAPHAEL SANTI

a very beautiful *Madonna with Christ and S. John*, had within his recollection been sold for a large price by the heirs of Taddeo to the Archduke Ferdinand Charles of Austria.

The Archduke was a son-in-law of Cosimo II., and his presence is recorded in Florence on a visit during a part of 1661 and 1662, and therefore the date at which the picture passed into his possession is narrowly defined by circumstances. He took it back with him to the castle of Innsbruck, and in 1663 it was removed to the château of Ambras, where it figures in an inventory:—'Unnser liebe Fraw, mit dem Nackhend steenden Christ Kindl vnnd vor Im St. Johannes knieend, beede das Kreuz haltend in einer vergulten Ramb auf Holz gemalen Original von Raphael da Urbino.'

In the year 1773 it was transferred to the Imperial Gallery at Vienna.

VIII

THE MADONNA DEL CARDELLINO

UFFIZI GALLERY, FLORENCE

THE *Madonna del Cardellino* or *Madonna of the Goldfinch* was painted by Raphael as a wedding present for Lorenzo Nasi, one of his intimate friends during the first years of his life in Florence. Our knowledge of the circumstance is due to Vasari. Nasi having, he says, taken a wife at that time, Raphael painted a picture for him, wherein he represented Our Lady with the Child between her knees, to whom a little S. John is joyously offering a bird, which is causing infinite delight and gladness to both the children. In the attitude of each, he continues, there is a certain childish simplicity which is quite adorable ; and they are moreover so admirably coloured, and finished with so much care, that they seem more like living beings than constructed by colours and design. The figure of Our Lady in like manner has an air of singular grace and divinity ; and, in fine, the foreground, the surrounding landscape, and all the other parts of the work are extremely beautiful.

The entry in a Florentine document, cited by Gronau, of the birth of a son Battista, on March 18th, 1506, to

Lorenzo Nasi and his wife Sandra di Matteo Canigiani, points to the marriage having taken place during the the first half of the year 1505. If therefore Raphael's wedding present to Lorenzo Nasi was even commenced at the time of his wedding, as appears probable, it seems natural to suppose that it was completed before the visit to Perugia, that is, in the course of the summer of 1505. Possibly, on account of the nature of the occasion for which it was painted, it may in the later stages of its execution have taken precedence over the *Madonna of the Meadow*, although the latter had been commenced before it. This may be the explanation of a certain difference of type discernible in the picture at Vienna and the shaded study for it at Oxford, to which reference has already been made as suggesting a difference in the time of execution. The *Madonna of the Meadow* may in fact be said to be at once more Peruginesque and more Leonardesque than the *Madonna of the Goldfinch*, which by contrast seems to mark the moment of Raphael's most complete absorption in the more purely Florentine art influences. Consequently, and perhaps more especially by design, in token of its occasion —the nature of which is appropriately symbolised by the white flowers in the foreground—the *Madonna of the Goldfinch* has a peculiar joyousness and idyllic note of rapture which distinguishes it among all the Madonnas of Raphael. It is exemplified in the benign, happy smile of the Virgin, from whose face, as she watches the children, love and joy seem to radiate like sunbeams,

The Madonna del Cardellino
Uffizi Gallery, Florence

THE MADONNA DEL CARDELLINO

while the happy play of the children fondling the bird, wherein, in contrast to the *Madonna of the Meadow* with its cross of reed, there is no token or foreshadowing of graver things, is like an idyll of spring untroubled of the seasons that follow.

The modelling of the body of the Child Christ is quite beyond praise, supple and firm of limb, yet deliciously soft and rounded, and the expression is exquisite in baby gravity. Firm with all the tension of life, S. John has run up like a little *amorino* who has just shot an arrow from his bow; but the spirit which dominates is not that of the antique, but Florentine of the Quattrocento. From Desiderio and Rossellino it has gathered something of its grace of plastic curve, but the greatest influence is that of Donatello. The S. John is one of the singing boys of the Cantoria translated into colour, keeping almost to the full his life and elasticity of limb. There is a like firmness of modelling and plastic grace in the figure of the Madonna, and some suggestion of Ghirlandaio in the structure of the head and in the treatment of the hair, which breaks at either side into ripples that seem like spray caught up from a wave by the off-shore breeze.

The group is set in relief against the warm brown tints of the ground and the soft haze of distance and sky. The landscape is Umbrian in arrangement, with the conventional aspen-like trees in the middle distance, but with an added softness of contour and power of space gradation. It is of great richness and diversity; a vision framed by the wooded Tuscan hills, where a bridge spans the foaming Arno, and Florence is seen in the far distance as a clear walled city with Brunelleschi's dome and aerial towers, and castle-crowned hills rising above it.

The landscape had a peculiar fitness in a gift to a Florentine, and the picture has never left the Tuscan country. The preparatory drawings for it are as numerous as those for the *Madonna of the Meadow*. The sequence of them reveals Raphael's indefatigable industry as impressively as any other group of his work. The incident from which the picture derives its name was only adopted after various other motives had been tried and dismissed, as not satisfying fully the artist's intention. In what is apparently one of the earliest of these studies the Virgin is represented reading a book, and the Child leaning on her knee is trying to reach it, S. John not being shown. This motive is preserved in the lesser of two sketches on a sheet in the University Galleries at Oxford (No. 47). In this the lines of the composition have become more rhythmical, and the figure of the Virgin has grown in statuesque grace. In a larger drawing on the same sheet, the Virgin, studied from an undraped model, is sitting, and has the Child seated on her lap, and S. John is standing by her side holding up a small bird, at which the Virgin and Christ are looking.

In this drawing, which is of great vigour, the motive which unites S. John to the group is not altogether satisfying, and the pyramidal form of composition has been abandoned by the change in the position

THE MADONNA DEL CARDELLINO

of the limbs of the Virgin, owing to her having the Child seated on her lap. Raphael therefore afterwards returned to the motive of the lesser sketch, which he repeated with some slight variations on a somewhat larger scale (University Galleries, Oxford, No. 48). Then developing the idea a stage further (No. 49), he restored the pyramidal form, and united the three figures by making the Child Christ stand between the knees of the Virgin, who, with head bending forward, is holding a book open on her lap, while Christ, whom apparently she is teaching to read, touches it with his hand extended, and to the left S. John stands by her side and looks at the book. Finally, in the composition of the picture, Raphael, by a happy flash of genius, has combined two of these motives. The Virgin has been teaching the Child to read, but the lesson has been interrupted, and the book is held aside in her left hand. S. John, who formerly was only a spectator of the lesson, and so placed as only to see the back of the book, has now become an actor in the scene. He has just run up breathless to show the infant Christ a goldfinch which he has caught, and Christ's hand, extended very much as it was in the study of the reading lesson, is stroking the head of the bird. The Virgin, whose right hand rests on the shoulder of S. John, is looking down with a kindly smile at the two children.

The early history of the picture is indicated in Vasari. It remained as a most cherished possession of the Nasi family, and in the year 1547, when the Nasi palace in the Via de' Bardi suddenly collapsed as the result of a landslip of the hill of S. Giorgio, the panel was buried in the ruins, and when discovered was found to be broken in several pieces. These were put together with marvellous skill by Battista, the son of the said Lorenzo, who was himself a great lover of art. It passed into the state collections of the Medici from the Gallery of Cardinal Carlo de' Medici in the year 1666.

IX

THE PORTRAIT OF RAPHAEL

UFFIZI GALLERY, FLORENCE

AMONG the very numerous collection of the portraits of painters by themselves which forms one of the unique attractions of the Gallery of the Uffizi at Florence, none corresponds more completely to the ideal which emanates from the painter's works, or is more entirely characteristic of what biographical records enable us to discern as to his personality than does that which bears the name of Raphael.

'A modest and gentle youth,' 'discreto e gentile giovane,' so the Duchess of Sora, Giovanna della Rovere, described him in the letter that she wrote to Pier Soderini, armed with which he arrived in Florence at the close of the year 1504. The characteristics are those which first meet the eye in the present work, executed in all probability during a visit paid to Urbino in the latter part of the year 1506, and showing in its air of pensive melancholy and in the clear olive flesh colouring such a recrudescence of sympathy with Umbrian methods as Raphael might naturally feel on revisiting his native city.

RAPHAEL SANTI

The similarity of type to that of the recumbent figure in the *Vision of a Knight* is such as to suggest the reading of a personal meaning into the allegory.

The panel has suffered considerably from bad usage, the colour on a part of the cheek would seem to have been scraped off and the modelling has suffered in consequence, and ill-judged restorations have impaired the delicacy of the line. But the soft, girlish beauty, the delicate, pensive air of melancholy and refinement mirrored in the face lend the picture a distinction quite apart from its subject.

It bears some resemblance in composition and the treatment of certain details, as the frizzly hair and the white frill of the doublet, to the portrait of *Angelo Doni*, which he had painted only a short time previously, and the clear olive colour of the flesh is of the same texture as that of the ' unknown lady ' of the Tribuna, attributed by some critics to Perugino, by others—as I think, more correctly—to Raphael.

The pallor of the face is the more marked by contrast with the dark background, the black cap and doublet, the dark, luxuriant chestnut hair, and the soft greyish hue of the panel.

It is indeed of striking beauty. A fine oval face, slender aquiline nose, eyes brown and deep set, and brows in a perfect arch above them ; mouth and nostrils very delicately drawn and seeming sensitive with life.

Contrast the portrait with another of a painter by himself—with that in red chalk by Leonardo in the Royal

The Portrait of Raphael
Uffizi Gallery, Florence

THE PORTRAIT OF RAPHAEL

Library at Turin, with the deep-set eyes and furrowed brow. It seems like that of a young page in the presence of a king. The wonder is enhanced that this stripling, so gentle and wistful, in so brief a span of life, seemed to bring all his dreams to birth. It has fixed for all time the traditional likeness of the painter, but the lack of corroborative evidence as to its origin has caused its authenticity as a portrait to be called in question. It is, however, in essential agreement with the figure in the *School of Athens* in which, according to tradition, the artist has represented himself, and also with the drawing in chalk in the University Galleries at Oxford of a boy of between fifteen and sixteen years of age, with a gentle and thoughtful expression and delicate features, which is believed to be a portrait of Raphael by Timoteo Viti, made when he was a pupil in Timoteo's studio at Urbino.

The panel remained at Urbino until the year 1588, when it is said to have been taken to Rome by Federigo Zuccaro, the first director of the Accademia di San Luca. It was afterwards acquired from the picture gallery of the Academy by Cardinal Leopold de' Medici when the latter formed the nucleus of the collection of portraits of painters which afterwards passed to the Uffizi. It is mentioned in 1675 in an inventory of the Cardinal's possessions.

X

THE MADONNA OF THE HOUSE OF ORLEANS

MUSÉE CONDÉ, CHANTILLY

'GREATER freedom and more vigorous movement,' so Wölfflin tersely defines the essential qualities of the Florentine ideal as distinct from that of Raphael, at the period at which he executed the *Madonna del Gran Duca*. The words serve admirably to characterise the line of development of the series of half-length figures of the Madonna with the Child, which followed one after another in rapid succession during the years of his residence in Florence, and culminated in the *Madonna della Sedia*. By contrast with the measure of realisation of this aim visible in the *Bridgewater*, *Colonna* and *Cowper Madonnas*, the *Madonna del Gran Duca* seems in design, though not in execution, to have a closer affinity with the pre-Florentine series. It breathes the Umbrian stillness; its successors reveal in a gathering fulness the intimacy and variety of life. In this series, the little cabinet picture known as the *The Madonna of the House of Orleans*, possesses a certain distinction in the fact that it represents the maximum extent of departure from precedent in arrangement.

MADONNA OF THE HOUSE OF ORLEANS

He has varied the angle of inclination of the figure of the Virgin, from the usual vertical position, so that head and shoulders are bending forward to a line parallel to that of the body of the Child, whom she is clasping round the shoulders with one hand while the other is extended to support the outstretched foot, as he lies on her lap, with hands stretched out as though clinging to the hem of her robe. This has made the composition rich in novel symmetry of functional lines, representing a scene of utmost intimacy combined with freedom and vigour of movement.

It is also unique among the Madonnas of Raphael in that the background shows a domestic interior. Morelli in speaking of this section of Raphael's work, in which ' the Madonna is humanised and becomes the tender mother,' refers to the landscape backgrounds as marking the moment at which Italian art steps out of the Church and seeks the open air. The *Madonna of the House of Orleans* registers a stage in the progress in which the new-found freedom is transferred to new surroundings. The Virgin is seated on a cushioned bench of a little room; behind her on the left is a curtain of a reddish grey material, on the right above her head is a shelf with a row of pots and a straw-plaited wine-flask; one of the former appears to be an apothecary's jar, another has a cover of parchment. So entirely is it conceived and executed in the spirit of *genre* painting, that Passavant supposed all the background to have been added later, Raphael having apparently left it in a dull uniform colour analogous to that of the *Madonna del Gran Duca*, and in a mood of creative adventure he ascribed the accessories, on stylistic grounds, to Teniers. But the shelf with pots on it, on which Passavant's supposition may not unfairly be described as resting, has been shown to have close analogies in contemporary art. A similar shelf occurs in a fresco by Filippino Lippi at S. Maria sopra Minerva in Rome, and also in that by Ghirlandaio in the Ognissanti at Florence which represents S. Jerome in his study. The latter work must undoubtedly have been known to Raphael personally, and it is not improbable that the shelf, which is in the same position as in the picture, and which, although more plenteously stocked with pots, contains several of an exactly similar shape, may have suggested the idea to him.

The face of the Virgin resembles that in the *Madonna of the Goldfinch* and *La Belle Jardinière* so closely that it is reasonable to suppose that Raphael made use of the same model for all three pictures. The Virgin is distinctively Florentine, both in type and treatment. The influence of Quattrocento sculpture is still discernible, but it is no longer dominant to the extent that it is in the *Tempi Madonna*. A certain additional simplicity and directness seems to suggest the influence of Ghirlandaio's great work in S. Maria Novella.

There is no direct evidence as to the time or circumstances of the origin of the picture, but the former is

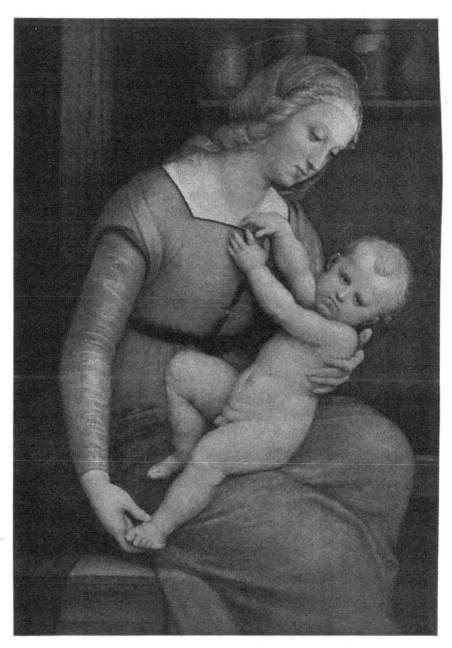

The Madonna of the House of Orleans
Musée Conde, Chantilly

MADONNA OF THE HOUSE OF ORLEANS

defined approximately by the similarity of the Virgin to the Virgin of *La Belle Jardinière* which bears the date 1507.

The picture is, however, generally assumed to be one of two Madonnas 'small but exceedingly beautiful and in his second manner,' which, according to Vasari, Raphael painted for Guidobaldo during a visit which he paid to Urbino in the year 1506. At the time that Vasari wrote, that is in 1568, the pictures were still at Urbino in the possession of the Duke. His description corresponds very closely to the Orleans Madonna.

An entry in an inventory at Urbino is quoted by Crowe and Calvalcaselle :—' Quadretto d'una Madonna con un Cristo in braccio in legno che viene da Raffaello.'

The early history of the picture is obscure. M. Gruyer's suggestion that it was once in Flanders and belonged to Teniers the younger rests apparently on the hypothesis of Passavant. The name is most probably derived from the fact that it belonged to the Gallery of the Regent Orleans, but the picture is said to have also been in the possession of Philip, Duke of Orleans, the brother of Louis XIV. The Orleans Gallery was removed to Brussels at the time of the French Revolution, and the Italian section, among which was Raphael's picture, was sold in London in 1798. After passing through the Hibbert, Vernon, Delamarre, Aguado and Delesser Collections, it was acquired in 1869 by the Duc d'Aumale, and since then it has formed part of the Musée Condé at Chantilly.

XI

S. GEORGE

HERMITAGE GALLERY, PETROGRAD

THE *S. George* in the Hermitage Gallery is the latest in order of composition of a number of small pictures, the dimensions of which are not more than about 12 inches by 10, all associated, either by tradition or on stylistic grounds, with the various occasions of Raphael's residence in Urbino.

The *Vision of a Knight* and the *S. Michael* in the Louvre were painted in all probability when he was still in close association with Timoteo Viti. The *S. George* in the Louvre and that in the Hermitage are connected with visits paid to his native city from Perugia and Florence. Vasari also mentions as works executed on his return from Florence two small Madonna pictures in his second manner, and a little panel of *Christ Praying in the Garden*. Apparently Guidobaldo had a predilection for cabinet pictures.

It might seem as though the memory of illuminated missal and manuscript seen in the famous Library at Urbino, where as a child Raphael must have often feasted curious eyes, during such time as Giovanni Santi was obtaining information for his *Rhyming Chronicle* from the

S. GEORGE

Duke Federigo's secretary and historian, Pierantonio Paltroni, came to exert a controlling influence over the work which he did in Urbino, giving it a closer affinity to the art of the miniaturist.

The influence is seen at its maximum in the *S. Michael*, which shares with the *Vision of a Knight* the claim to be regarded as the earliest extant specimen of Raphael's work. Morelli gives it the priority. The figure of the saint is more vigorous in conception than any in the *Vision*, but it is far more open to criticism in the structure. The right thigh is much too short, and the balance of the body is quite unconvincing.

Entirely in the spirit of book illustration is the circle of grotesque fiends in the middle distance, and also the sulphurous city of Dis and the groups of sinners undergoing punishment. There is something Dantesque in the conception, with an added touch of necromancy, which, as Crowe and Cavalcaselle suggest, may have been derived from one of the prints of Jerome Bosch.

The dry, hard browns of the foreground, entirely in keeping with the scene, have given place to an altogether different scheme of colour in the companion picture of the *S. George*, also in the Louvre. Here both in the arrangement and in the treatment of the landscape, with its subtle harmony of greys and greens and the far vista seen through graceful aspens, the influence of Perugino is marked. That Raphael returned to Urbino before proceeding to Florence after his association with Perugino in Perugia and his work in Città di Castello, is clearly to be inferred from the fact of Giovanna della Rovere, the mother of the heir to the duchy, having written at Urbino, in October 1504, a letter for him to present to the Gonfaloniere of Florence, Pier Soderini. To the period of this visit the *S. George* of the Louvre is to be assigned on stylistic grounds.

Lomazzo says that Raphael painted a picture of *S. George* for the Duke of Urbino. A record tells how, in the Carnival of the year 1504, the peril of the Borgia invasion of the Duchy of the previous year was made a scenic spectacle for the revels of the Montefeltrian court. It is natural to assume in Raphael's picture a reference to the same series of events, St. George slaying the dragon being his allegory of the Duke's triumph over his enemies the Borgias. Returning to Urbino two years later from Florence, Raphael painted the three small pictures mentioned by Vasari, one of which may be identified with the *Orleans Madonna*; he also painted another *S. George* for the Duke, that now in the Hermitage Gallery.

A silver-point drawing at Oxford (University Galleries, No. 35), in which the angle of direction of the horse is so altered that the saint is galloping away from the spectator instead of towards him, contains the germ of the second composition as distinct from the first. The reversal of the position of horse and rider was first suggested by the study of the bas-relief of Donatello's statue in Or Sanmichele. The influence of the work of Donatello is seen in all the Florentine works of Raphael in the enhanced vitality of modelling. A study of the statue

S. George
Hermitage Gallery, Petrograd

S. GEORGE

in Or Sanmichele occurs in a drawing of a group of warriors (Oxford University Galleries). On returning to the *S. George* composition, after becoming acquainted with the bas-relief, he transferred many of its essential details, assimilating them so completely that the work seems to be conceived and executed in natural sequence to the series of cabinet pictures, combining their miniature-like fidelity with an added freedom and boldness of composition. Raphael's final cartoon for the Hermitage picture, in the Uffizi, pricked for transfer to the panel, shows the extent of his indebtedness even more completely than does the picture itself.

The princess is placed farther in the background in the picture than in the bas-relief, and is kneeling in prayer instead of standing, but the upper part of the figure is closely derived from it, as also is the position of the knight, seen from behind, in full armour, with low round helmet and mantle streaming in the wind, as he bends forward on his spear and deals the death-stroke. By reversing the attitude of the body of the dragon from that in the bas-relief, he has created new parallels of line which accentuate the impression of the speed of the horse. Its position is founded upon the bas-relief, but the hind legs are extended as galloping. The great increase in power in the composition of the horse, as compared either with the bas-relief or Raphael's earlier picture, may be ascribed to the study of Leonardo's cartoon for the 'Battle of the Standard,' which the painter was at work upon in the Sala del Consiglio during

RAPHAEL SANTI

Raphael's first years in Florence. His interest in this work is borne testimony to by Vasari, and the vitality of the head of the charger is such as to establish its lineage with the work of Leonardo, in which, as sundry early copies and a drawing made by Rubens serve to show, the horses were represented as sharing in the frenzy of combat.

Below the left knee of the rider is a blue garter on which the word 'honi' is visible. This being the commencement of the device of the Order of St. George, its appearance in this picture is naturally connected with the fact that the order was conferred upon Guidobaldo by Henry VII. in the summer of 1504, on the occasion of an embassy from the English king to Pope Julius, he having been selected for the honour, which had also been conferred upon his father, on account probably of his position as commander of the papal army.

By the rules of the order it was incumbent upon the newly appointed knight to send a representative within eight months in order to receive investiture, and to this office the Duke designated Baldassare Castiglione, who speaks of his forthcoming journey in a letter of May 1505. Castiglione's journey was, however, deferred for a year through illness. He set out on July 10th, 1506. His journey to London, his reception by the king, his subsequent visits to the various knights of the order are all recorded with appropriate circumstance. What concerns us more nearly is that among the various presents from the Duke of Urbino to Henry VII. which Castiglione took with him was a small picture of *S. George* by Raphael.

Passavant, Crowe and Cavalcaselle, Gronau and others have all concluded that this was the picture now in the Hermitage, the garter and the motto being held apparently to establish the identification. It is, however, quite as likely that Raphael would thus decorate a picture which was intended to remain in the possession of a newly appointed knight of the order, as that he would be called upon to do so to one which was to be sent as a present to the monarch who bestowed the order.

Castiglione's journey being delayed for a year by illness, it is natural to suppose that the presents were ready at the time at which it was first intended that the journey should take place. The probability that the picture was ready to be sent in the summer of 1505 points strongly to it as being the version now in the Louvre, which has every indication of being anterior to the time of Raphael's residence in Florence. Similarly, the evidence of the study of the Donatello bas-relief, visible in the Hermitage picture, renders it very improbable that it could have been executed by the summer of 1505.

The conclusion to which all these considerations point is confirmed by a note found in an Inventory of the possessions of King Henry VIII., to whom the picture passed by succession from Henry VII. This Inventory (British Museum, Harleian MS., 1419) in the section 'Stuffe and Inplumentes at Westminster' specifies (f. 130) 'a Table with the picture of saincte George his speare beinge broken and his sworde in his hande.' This clearly can only have reference to the picture in the Louvre, which has the broken spear and the sword in the hand of the saint. In the version at the Hermitage the saint has a spear in his hand, which is not broken, and his sword hangs by his side. It follows therefore that the earlier picture, now in the Louvre, was the one which Guidobaldo sent to England, and that the picture at the Hermitage was commissioned as a substitute for it, in which, in compliment to the Duke's recent distinction, Raphael introduced the garter and the motto of the order on the knee of the warrior saint.

The *S. George* in the Louvre, after having been in the possession of Henry VII. and Henry VIII., passed out of the royal collections at some date unknown. The next record of it is found in the inventory of the Gallery of Cardinal Mazarin, who died in 1661. It then passed into the possession of Louis XIV. and so into the Louvre Collections.

The *S. George* in the Hermitage Gallery was also brought to England at some period after it had passed out of the Urbino collections, and was acquired by the Earls of Pembroke; and in 1627, while in their collection, it was engraved in reverse by Vorsterman. A reproduction of the engraving is given in Sir Claude Phillips' monograph on the Collection of Charles I.

In Vanderdoort's catalogue of King Charles I.'s pictures there is an entry of 'a little St. George, which

S. GEORGE

the king had in exchange of My Lord Chamberlain, Earl of Pembroke, for the book of Holbein's drawings.'

The engraving by Vorsterman establishes incontestably the identity of the Hermitage picture with that in the collection of the Earl of Pembroke: unless we suppose Vanderdoort to have confused the two pictures, his evidence shows that it was the Hermitage picture which was in the collection of Charles I., and which, after his execution, was sold for £150 by the orders of the Commonwealth.

Not less unmistakably does the entry in the record of Henry VIII.'s pictures refer to the Louvre composition. It would therefore seem natural to conclude—giving due weight to each of the two pieces of evidence—that both the Louvre composition of *S. George* and that in the Hermitage Gallery have at one time formed part of the English Royal Collections.

M. Somof, in the Official Catalogue of the Hermitage, states that the picture there was acquired by M. de la Noue, who afterwards ordered Philipe de Champaigne to make a copy of it.

As Philipe de Champaigne died in 1674, aged seventy-two, this establishes the location of the picture at about the middle of the seventeenth century, or very shortly after the sale of Charles I.'s pictures, which took place in 1649. The subsequent owners are stated to have been the Marquis de Sourdis, Baron de Crozat and Baron Thiers. In 1771 the picture was bought by the Empress Catherine II. of Russia.

XII

THE ENTOMBMENT

BORGHESE GALLERY, ROME

A RECENT writer on Raphael—M. Gillet—has made the computation that among the various collections of his drawings there are a hundred which are to be considered as preparatory studies for the *Entombment*. No other work of Raphael's—very few by any artist—has been preceded by such a long continuity of ordered effort. While the result is justly extolled as a triumph of the academic, in that he brought to bear such resolution as compelled success, it none the less reveals —more fully perhaps than any other work—how essentially derivative and assimilative was his art so soon as it moved away from the region of reverie and allegory, in which—true Umbrian as he was—expression seemed intuitive, and adventured upon the wider fields of human action and emotion.

There the subject led him inevitably, when called upon to memorialise Atalanta Baglione's grief for her son in the expiatory chapel which she had caused to be erected in S. Francesco. For Raphael had been in Perugia at the time of the Baglione massacres, when Grifonetto had murdered Astorre and his household, gathered together at

THE ENTOMBMENT

a marriage feast, and had thus brought upon himself condign vengeance from their common kinsman, Giovan Paolo. He had known how Atalanta had refused to recognise the murderer as her son, and then had gone back to him on hearing that he had suffered the due punishment for his crime, and as the price of her blessing had obtained that his last words as he lay dying were of forgiveness to his own assassin. It was about six years after—if we accept the order of sequence of events as narrated by Vasari—when Raphael had gone to Perugia from Florence in order to paint a fresco of the Trinity in S. Severo, on which occasion he also did several other works, that Atalanta Baglioni invited him to undertake the commission. He offered in reply to prepare the cartoon in Florence, whither he was then on the point of returning, and execute it on the first convenient opportunity. It was therefore with a more than usual feeling of freedom of time and occasion that he set out to explore the possibilities of the subject. In inception his standpoint, as ever, was Umbrian. A Pietà which by analogy should eternise Atalanta's sorrow clothed itself naturally in facile Peruginesque formulas. But there is something of that added touch of simplicity and sincerity which he always imparted to the Peruginesque in a drawing with the pen at Oxford (Univ. Galleries, No. 37), which preserves what was apparently his first conception.

The debt to Perugino's treatment of the same subject now in the Pitti, executed in 1495, for the nuns of Santa Chiara at Florence, is such, both in general structure and in individual types, as to argue his complete familiarity either with the painting or the various studies for it.

In a pen-drawing in the Louvre (No. 319), a study carried to a very high degree of finish, closely connected in composition with the sketch at Oxford, and separated from it only by a short though fruitful interval, the number of characters has been reduced from ten to eight, and there is more effort of concentration, but the influences perceptible have become more varied.

As in the Oxford sketch, the influence of Perugino is still dominant, and certain of the figures are moulded upon those in the Santa Chiara picture, but there are also traces visible of the immature attempt to follow out certain of Leonardo's precepts, which have caused some exaggeration of emphasis of pose and gesture in certain of the figures gathered round the body of Christ, as though every hand must needs arrest the eye by the significance of its action. Of the group of four in the Oxford drawing, standing on the right as spectators, one only is left, and in the dramatic expression of this figure gazing with clenched hands uplifted, and in a certain statuesque quality of pose, there is so close a resemblance to the figure similarly placed in Mantegna's print of the 'Entombment' as to warrant the assumption that he derived assistance from it.

Mr. Dryhurst, in his study of Raphael, puts forward the very reasonable suggestion that it was his study of this print, first revealed in this figure in the Louvre Pietà, that caused him to alter the time of action which he had chosen

The Entombment
Borghese Gallery, Rome

THE ENTOMBMENT

for representation, in the sacred history. In all subsequent drawings connected with the subject Raphael is preparing an *Entombment*.

Roused to emulation by the monumental lines of Mantegna's print, of which a study occurs in the so-called Venetian Sketch Book, and taking as the basis of his new composition its central arrangement of the figures carrying the body of Christ, he essayed the problem of movement, and followed this new vista, as his manner was, by careful study of muscle and sinew held taut and in action, and of the structure of the frame beneath. It is natural to connect with these studies, which are numerous, the testimony of Vasari as to his late attention to the anatomical study of the nude, by which he divested himself of the manner practised by Perugino. Not only Mantegna, but Signorelli also, and Michelangelo, each of whom set himself to interpret in his manner that exuberance of strength of the human form which gives the limbs in repose infinite suggestion of movement, yielded something to his eager search; the result is apparent in a drawing with the pen in the Uffizi of the figures of the bearers which apparently served for the central part of the cartoon for the picture. Another drawing, formerly in the Malcolm Collection, preserves his design for the Madonna amid her women, which in the picture has taken the place of the isolated figure that first attracted him in Mantegna's print; in another in the same collection this new anatomical zeal has caused him to draw a skeleton in the position occupied by the Virgin. In the picture this excess of study and preparation, perhaps also the change of purpose, have caused a certain lack of unity in result.

There are the mourners. The Magdalen in an agony of grief is seizing the hand of Christ. S. John in the background bending forward is gazing at him; the figure is almost identical with that in the Oxford drawing for a Pietà. The Virgin has relinquished her place beside the body, and has fallen in a swoon in the arms of her women. Against this background of types charged with mental emotion, is the sharply contrasted factor of physical effort in the figures of the two men, who, with the help of Joseph of Arimathea, have lifted up the body of Christ and are about to mount the steps leading to the sepulchre.

These, who have dispossessed the mourners, bring to their office no solemnity of thought. One body is as another, and they are mere physical machines set in motion, Raphael having allowed his new-found interest in the dynamical laws which govern the act to infringe somewhat upon the nature of the theme. Their prototypes are the bearers in Mantegna's print, which was the primary source of his composition. They are gaunt and stern as Mantegna's Roman soldiers, with muscles strong as bands of iron. Something also has gone to their making from the more deeply purposed and subtly modelled nudes in the cartoon of the 'Bathers,' made by Michelangelo in the Council Chamber, which shared with that of Leonardo the title of 'The School of the World.' Following on the counsels and practice of

THE ENTOMBMENT

both, Raphael drew this part with nude figures that he might study the action and strain of muscle. To the influence of Michelangelo and Fra Bartolommeo may be assigned the functional quality of the grouping of the women round the Virgin. To the former may be traced the suggestion of the figure of the woman who kneels supporting the Virgin, which is derived from the 'Holy Family,' which he made for Angelo Doni, at whose house Raphael may have studied it, and the figure of Christ shows a close analogy to that in the Pietà in S. Peter's at Rome. To the examples and precepts of Fra Bartolommeo and Leonardo may be ascribed the quality of *sfumato* visible in the modelling of the figures.

Raphael was great enough to borrow as he listed, as did Shakespeare, but his true strength lay more within himself than in the lines along which he followed in the *Entombment*. In the case of his more immediate contemporaries, he borrowed the letter without the spirit, and in the result there is not that entire assimilation which makes his work seem the natural and ultimate expression of those painters of the Quattrocento whose work he studied. Lacking this, the *Entombment* seems an academic exercise. As such it reveals the wonderful dexterity of his art.

On the step in the left the picture bears the inscription—

RAPHAEL . VRBINAS . M.D.VII.

It remained at Perugia in the church of S. Francesco until the year 1608, when it was removed secretly by the monks and sent to Pope Paul V., who bestowed it upon his kinsman, Cardinal Scipio Borghese, the founder of the Borghese Gallery. In company with so many works of art, it was removed to Paris in 1797, and was given back in 1815, since when it has remained in the Borghese Gallery.

A lunette, with a half length of *God the Father*, surrounded by eleven small angels added by a later hand, is still in the church at Perugia.

The predella, which consists of symbolic representations of the three theological virtues, Faith, Charity and Hope, with an angel on either side of each, painted in grisaille on a grey background, presents a very attractive instance of the softness of contour and delicacy of modelling of his work of the Florentine period. It remained at Perugia until the year 1797, when it was taken to Paris. Since its return to Italy in 1815 it has remained in the Vatican Gallery.

XIII

THE MADONNA OF THE HOUSE OF ALBA

HERMITAGE GALLERY, PETROGRAD

AS the lessons of his Umbrian training are predominant in some of the works which Raphael executed after his arrival in Florence, so Florentine influences continued to supply the keynotes of some of the works of his Roman period. While in the Vatican he was immersed in new problems of space composition, the Madonnas which were the product of his spare hours carried on the old traditions more closely.

The *Madonna of the House of Alba* which is appaently the ultimate expression of that pyramidal composition of the Virgin with the infant Christ and S. John, derived originally from the precepts of the art-schools of Florence, was executed soon after Raphael's arrival in Rome. The fact that a sheet of preparatory studies for it in red chalk in the Wicar Museum at Lille also contains studies for the *Madonna della Sedia* and for the Child in the *Bridgewater Madonna*, the latter composition being entirely Florentine in spirit, while the former, on stylistic grounds, must be assigned to the latter half of the Roman period, illustrates the difficulty of attempting to rest chronological conclusions on such evidence.

The Roman origin of the picture is to be inferred from the treatment of the drapery of the Virgin, with its free suggestion of the antique, in the added richness of the material of her dress, in her sandals, and in the statuesque pose of both Mother and Child, who have nevertheless the full freedom of action. It is seen also in the landscape, which, according to Passavant and Crowe and Cavalcaselle, is typical of the banks of the Tiber. There is a breadth and spaciousness about it which are altogether different from the Arno scene in the *Madonna del Cardellino*. A more positive indication may perhaps be found in the fact that sprigs with oak leaves are growing from the trunk against which the Madonna is leaning, which may be an allusion to the picture as having been a commission for a patron of the Rovere family.

The Florentine note is no less distinct. It is more fundamental, although it reveals itself primarily in Raphael's attempt to assimilate the characteristic features of the work of his contemporaries. In this case the attempt reveals his limitations. As in the *Entombment*, where his own natural clarity of vision seems clouded and obscured by the pertinacity of his efforts to grasp the secret of Michelangelo's power to suggest titanic energy and deep emotion by the natural structure and movement of the limbs, so here he seems to be essaying the less onerous task of translating Michelangelesque depth of feeling to the more familiar

THE MADONNA OF THE HOUSE OF ALBA

subject of the Madonna, choosing naturally for the purpose the form of the *tondo*, preferred by Michelangelo in his treatment of the Madonna. With some apparent conflict of purpose he strives to capture at the same time something of the softness and subtilty of expression of Leonardo. Each was as the bow of Ulysses, and Raphael, who, in his single achievement, gathered up and perfected the art tenets of Umbria and of Florence of the Quattrocento, strove in vain to bend it.

There is a certain exaggeration of emphasis most noticeable in the figure of the infant Christ, who is described by Crowe and Cavalcaselle as 'half climbing, half gliding on the lap of the Virgin, clinging to her whilst he turns to grasp at the stem of the cross to which his glance is directed.' The Virgin and apparently S. John are also looking at it. The motive is almost the same as in the *Madonna of the Meadow*, but the note of foreboding is almost strident by contrast. The figure of the Virgin, who, with one leg extended and the other bent beneath her, is leaning on her elbow against the trunk of a tree, has been carefully studied in the drawing in red chalk at Lille, and the figure is repeated on the reverse of the sheet with a youth as model. Raphael has completely triumphed over the difficulties of balance in what was an unusual attitude, but the artificiality is inherent in the pose. The angles of direction of the figure are apparently modelled on those of Leonardo in the 'Madonna with S. Anne,' which Raphael must have studied at Florence. The same influence may be held to account for the modelling of the head and neck of the Virgin. These attempt an expressiveness almost alien to the simpler, firmer structure of the figure as indicated in the studies at Lille.

Other studies connected with it are a sketch in the Albertina and two cartoons. One of these in black chalk is in the sacristy of S. Giovanni in Laterano at Rome; the other in sepia, in the collection of the Counts of Outremont at Liége, may possibly be identical with a cartoon referred to by Crowe and Cavalcaselle as having formerly been in the church of the Knights of Malta at Gaeta, there described in the registers as a copy.

At the time of the earliest record the picture was in the church of the monastery of Monte Oliveto at Nocera de' Pagani in the province of Naples. Paolo Giovio, the art collector and historian, the writer of the earliest biography of Raphael, who is said to have stimulated Vasari to write the *Lives of the Artists*, was made bishop of Nocera by Clement VII. and Passavant makes the reasonable suggestion that it was through him that the monastery of Monte Oliveto came into possession of the picture. It is mentioned as being in the church in 1623 by the historian of the order, and in 1686, the date being established by a recently discovered document, it was purchased from the monks by the Viceroy of Naples, the Marchese del Caprio. When his term of service was expired, he took the picture with him to Spain, where it subsequently passed into the possession of the Dukes of Alva or Alba, in whose palace at

THE MADONNA OF THE HOUSE OF ALBA

Madrid it was seen and described in 1793. The gallery also contained a very good copy of the picture, and at the end of the century both the original and the copy were bequeathed by a Duchess of Alba to her physician as a token of gratitude for her recovery from an illness. Her sudden death, which took place very soon afterwards, caused the physician to be arrested on the charge of administering poison, but he was acquitted through the influence of Godoy, to whom he afterwards presented the copy.

The original picture was sold by the physician to the Danish ambassador, Count Edmond Bourke. Bourke soon afterwards was transferred to London, and there sold it to a dealer named Coesvelt, from whom it was acquired in 1836 by the Czar Nicholas for the Hermitage Collection.

XIV

THE PARNASSUS

STANZA DELLA SEGNATURA, VATICAN

THE decoration of the Stanza della Segnatura was Raphael's first great work in Rome. From the letter which he wrote to Francia from Rome, dated September 5th, 1508, thanking him for the gift of his portrait, and excusing himself for not sending his own because he had not been able to get it done owing to his incessant labours, we may infer that the work had then already been commenced. The date 1511, inscribed below the *Parnassus*, shows when it was brought to a conclusion. These three years constitute the central period of Raphael's artistic life. They also mark the zenith of achievement. On the four walls of the room he has symbolised the history of the human intellect more comprehensively and with greater impressiveness than has ever been attempted by any other painter. The four medallions on the ceiling on which he has painted allegorical figures representing Theology, Philosophy, Poetry and Justice, serve as an induction to the scenes below—the *Disputa*, the *School of Athens*, the *Parnassus* and the *Allegory of Prudence* with the scenes of the *Giving of the Pandects* and the *Decretals*. Nothing in his previous work, either at Florence or in Umbria, can be looked upon as foretelling this performance. As yet principally a painter of cabinet pictures and altarpieces—Madonnas and allegories—he here passes with a stride to deal in ordered harmony with great spaces and with masses of men, revealing himself thereby as one of the greatest masters in the art of what Mr. Berenson has termed space-composition. In the imaginative representations which cover the walls of the Sala della Segnatura, by contrast with those more purely historical ones which he afterwards designed and in part executed in various other rooms of the Vatican, the rendering of the individual is entirely subordinate to the general conception. The figures present types, not portraits. The resultant harmony of lines, masses and colours creates so vivid an impression of beauty as to overpower and lead captive the emotions of the beholder, before ever the understanding has had time to interpret the forms thus presented. These aim at expressing the fulness of the heritage of the Renaissance, co-ordinating in a common purpose of endeavour classical, mediæval and contemporary types in the fields of theology and poetry, while in philosophy the pre-eminence of Greek thought is recognised in the exclusion of other schools.

Despite the testimony of Vasari, which in this instance is singularly confused, the *Disputa* must on stylistic grounds be considered the earliest of the series. It is entirely Umbro-Florentine in spirit. Its prototype is the upper part of the Trinity in S. Severo at Perugia, which Raphael painted about four years previously, with some temporary recrudescence of Peruginesque feeling.

The greater luminosity and atmospheric subtilty, and the added richness of expression, are a measure of the progress which had resulted from the years of study in Florence. The dominant influence is Fra Bartolommeo, to whose geometrical principles of grouping as seen in his 'Last Judgment,' now in the Uffizi, may be traced the entirely symmetrical arrangement of Raphael's types of the Church Triumphant.

In the *School of Athens* in the assemblage which throngs the foreground of a lofty Renaissance palace this symmetry has become ordered freedom. The *Disputa* displayed a consciousness of dawning power; but it is in the *School of Athens* that Raphael has broken the last link which bound him to the art of the Quattrocento. The expansion of style which the two works reveal is due in part to the spectacle of Michelangelo's frescoes in the Sistine Chapel, in part to the opportunities which Rome afforded for the study of the antique. The two influences have had some share in the dignity and freedom which characterise the figures, in the monumental treatment of the draperies, and the subordination of the action of the various individuals to the air of repose which pervades the whole.

Each of the two remaining walls is broken in its lower half by the projection of a window. In the upper half of one Raphael has symbolised the essential attributes of justice by three female figures who are repre-

THE PARNASSUS

sented as seated, playing with *amorini*; their beauty and grace of line bear traces of the study of the antique. On either side of the window below are representations of two great ceremonial events in the history of law; these form the earliest examples of his Roman work in portraiture, and already the note of realism is dominant. The *Giving of the Decretals*, in which Gregory IX. has the lineaments of Julius II., is based upon Melozzo da Forli's similarly arranged portrait group in the Vatican. The interest which Raphael would naturally feel in this piece of Quattrocento realism was enhanced by the memory of the painter's relations with Giovanni Santi, Melozzo being referred to in the *Rhyming Chronicle* in terms which betoken personal intimacy.

On the wall of the *Parnassus* he treated the whole surface as one, so arranging his composition that the projecting window serves only to enhance the effect of height of the hill of the Muses, the summit of which is placed immediately above it, while the slopes in the foreground descend on either side of the window.

On the hill-top, beneath a grove of laurel thrown into fine relief against a clear sky, is seated Apollo, and round about him are the Muses. It is not without significance that, whereas the symbolical figure of Poetry in the medallion on the ceiling above holds the classic lyre, Apollo is playing a violin, as he is in the picture which Timoteo Viti made for the series of Apollo and the Muses, which decorated the Library at Urbino. Both figures also have in common a certain Ferrarese suggestion in structure and handling. Timoteo Viti's creation is as frankly romantic in feeling as any of those of Dosso Dossi, and this mood was prevalent in the mind of Raphael when he created the *Parnassus*. It is a vision of softly tempered light and shadow, vibrant with colour. The conception is at least as much Italian as antique. But he is not concerned personally with things of time or place. It were vain to attempt to better the eloquent words of M. Gillet; 'Nous sommes ici hors des temps, dans le royaume des songes; ou plutôt, c'est le songe du siècle, c'est l'utopie de la Renaissance. Cet Eden, ce n'est pas la montagne de Phocide, c'est quelque jardin d'Italie, quelque terrasse de Mantoue, de Ferrare ou d'Urbin, où des dames et des cavaliers font le rêve d'une humanité heureuse en paix avec elle-même, en harmonie avec la Nature et la Grâce. C'est une scène du *Cortegiano* ou des *Asolani*. Entre le monde païen et le monde chrétien, le Parnasse propose sa cime conciliante; ainsi deux pays qui s'opposent par leurs vallées et le cours de leurs eaux, se rejoignent par leurs sommets.'

How admirably in the upturned eyes and parted lips of the god he has contrived to suggest the divine frenzy which the strains evoke! How fully this is reflected in the doting face of the Muse Erato, who sits with her lyre to the right of the god, gazing at him, or in the eager look of Clio behind, book in hand, and in Thalia, who is holding her mask! It produces also the *abandon* of unconscious delight which causes Terpsichore and Polyhymnia to cling fondly to each other, the one resting her head on the other's shoulder. The study of the antique accounts for some part of the plastic firmness and freedom of modelling which have given such charm to these clinging forms of Muses and to the figure of Apollo; but where the influence of the antique is most complete, as in the Muse Calliope seated on the left of the god, whose figure is an adaptation from a statue of Ariadne in the Vatican, the result is by contrast laboured and perfunctory. The other figures are modelled more on Renaissance types. They have lineage of Ferrara and Florence, with that added freedom and elasticity of pose won from the antique which the opportunities of study in Rome gave to his art.

The writers of great verse, as one of their number has said, are 'a little clan.' Raphael places less than a score of figures on the sacred mountain, and of these only three who form the group nearest to the god possess clearly recognisable characteristics. Homer, a majestic figure in whose features some resemblance may be traced to those of the Laocoon, stands with uplifted head singing in ecstasy to the music of Apollo. He alone, the father of all, partakes of the frenzy of the god. Nearest to him are Virgil and Dante, and by their side a youth is sitting ready to write down the words as they fall from Homer's lips. Just behind is another figure, unidentified, apparently a portrait. The group is balanced by one on the other side somewhat lower down the slope of the hill; there are also groups in the foreground on either side of the window. In one of these Sappho is discernible by her scroll. Petrarch, Tasso and Boccaccio may also be identified with more or less probability, and Vasari has attempted the identification of all the others. But it would seem to be little better than guess-work. By the omission of any identifying symbols or chronological marks of costume Raphael seems to be emphasising the importance of generalisation in monumental painting. His conception demonstrates the essential unity of the art of poetry in antiquity and in the time of the Renaissance. No greater tribute has ever been paid by one art to another than in this vision of Parnassus. Whether in conception it owed anything to the scheme of Petrarch's *Trionfi*, or to the counsels of such friends as Castiglione or Bembo, no evidence avails to aid to a conclusion. Such conjectures are facile; we are on surer ground in giving due weight to the fact that Raphael's nascent thoughts grew and expanded amid influences no less literary than artistic. All the years of Raphael's childhood Giovanni Santi was at work upon his poem which commemorated the deeds of the Duke Federigo. It is a thing of echoes where it has a clear sound at all, and the source of inspiration is, of course, the *Divina Commedia*. It opens in allegory with a vision seen in sleep, and such an allegory is the motive of what is perhaps Raphael's earliest work. It is somewhat late to suggest identifications where no new evidence offers in support; but it is perhaps not altogether fantastic to conjecture that in the introduction of the figure seen on the hill by the side of Dante, differing apparently from the other unidentified figures in that it seems designedly a portrait, and bearing a somewhat close resemblance in pose and type of features to Raphael's portrait of himself in the Uffizi, he may have ventured to pay a debt of filial piety to the author of the *Rhyming Chronicle*!

Crowe and Cavalcaselle enumerate six sheets of studies for various figures in the *Parnassus* at Windsor, at Lille, in the Albertina and at Oxford. Four of these have sketches on both sides of the page. One of those in the Albertina is the study for the Muse Calliope, the lines of which are adapted from the statue of Ariadne in the Vatican which was only discovered in the reign of Julius II. To the list may be added a drawing in the British Museum, a study of the drapery and the hands of the so-called Horace—the figure in the foreground on the extreme right. Oxford has also a copy by a pupil of a study for the arrangement of the figures in the upper part of the work.

The almost entire absence of alternative motives in the drawings connected with the *Parnassus* is an eloquent testimony to the sureness of his power of conception during the Roman period. If such variants of purpose had ever existed they would in all probability have been preserved. After the execution of the *Entombment*, over which his purpose was continually changing, he seems to have gained new facility of touch; from that time onward the hand moved more surely to register the creative impulse of the brain.

XV

THE PORTRAIT OF JULIUS II

UFFIZI GALLERY, FLORENCE

THE earliest of Raphael's numerous representations of Pope Julius II., occurs in the fresco in the Stanza della Segnatura of the *Giving of the Decretals by Gregory IX.*, who has the lineaments of the Rovere pope. He also is introduced in two of the frescoes in the Stanza of Heliodorus upon which Raphael was engaged between 1511 and 1514. In that representing the *Expulsion of Heliodorus from the Temple* he is shown on the left borne on his chair, a stern, wrathful figure, whose face embodies something of the divine vengeance of which he watches the enactment. In the *Mass of Bolsena*, which is the last of the works in the Vatican to bear the impress of Raphael's own hand in its execution, Julius is shown as Pope Urban IV., who kneels facing the officiating priest on the dais on which the miracle has taken place. There is the same grim tenacity of purpose, but the lines of the face are deeper and the expression is somewhat more passive. We may suppose it to represent the pontiff shortly before his death, which took place on the 20th of February 1513.

The Portrait of Julius II
Uffizi Gallery, Florence

THE PORTRAIT OF JULIUS II.

The order of the panel portrait of Julius II. in the series is established by the statement of Vasari, that it was undertaken at about the time when Raphael had completed the works in the one room at the Vatican and had received the commission for the second. It may therefore be assigned to the year 1511.

It is probably the earliest example still in existence of the series of portraits which Raphael painted at Rome, in which he showed power to delineate character to an extent to which his earlier work affords neither parallel nor promise. Whereas in the Florentine and earlier efforts in portraiture he seems always to be following some influence or convention, which in either case serves as a veil between the artist and the personality of the sitter, at Rome his vision became more direct and piercing. The Julius II. marks a stage in realism. Vasari describes the picture, which, when he wrote, was hanging in the Church of Santa Maria del Popolo, as possessing such animation and being so true to life that it filled the beholders with a sense of awe, just as did the Pope himself when he was alive.

It is the most dramatic in quality of presentment of any of Raphael's portraits. It communicates the effect of vigour and strength of personality by impressive simplicity of line and colour so potently, and with such mastery of technique, that of all the many representations of the Popes only the red 'Innocent X.' of Velasquez in the Doria Gallery can be adjudged its superior.

Giuliano della Rovere was one of the most imperious

and commanding figures who have ever occupied the papal throne. His prepossessions were those of the military leader. It is recorded that on being asked by Michelangelo whether in the bronze statue of himself which the sculptor was making for Bologna he would wish to be represented with a book in his left hand, his quick reply was, 'No, No! give me a sword, I am no scholar.' Whatever his attitude to letters—and great names were found among his Court—he was a munificent patron of art. He had an instinct tantamount to genius for choosing out the greatest artists of his age, and employing them upon such works as should call into being their highest powers. In like manner the great *condottieri* made their capitals art treasuries. Force and diplomacy, menace and political intrigue, were the weapons which he found most effective to assert the influence and increase the possessions of the Papacy. Like all the Italian princes of his time, he intrigued to bring foreign powers into Italy in order to serve his ends, and found himself playing with edged tools.

The beard which appears in all Raphael's portraits of him serves for a witness of this. He had resolved in the autumn of 1510 to let it grow until he should have expelled the French from Italy; after having sixteen years before, as a Cardinal in exile at the French court, been one of the prime movers in the bringing about the expedition of Charles VIII. His energy proved potent to effect his purpose, but at the period of this portrait he sat, as Crowe and Cavalcaselle put it, ' not as a chief

THE PORTRAIT OF JULIUS II.

elated with victory, but as one humbled by reverses.' He seems moody and troubled as he sits bent with cares. The eyes—set in deep hollows under the massive forehead—are full of singular fire and energy. The firm lines of the mouth, the furrowed brows, and the look of concentration of purpose which the features impart, build up a remarkable effect of vigour of character. It is the head of a dogged fighter—a natural leader in the world of action—and the breadth and suavity of treatment which are here displayed show how potent were the influences of naturalism of the opening years of Raphael's life at Rome.

Soon after the date at which Vasari wrote, the portrait was removed from the Church of S. Maria del Popolo together with the *Madonna* picture by Raphael which he described as then with it. It apparently returned into the possession of the della Rovere family. On the death of the last della Rovere Duke of Urbino in 1631, among the art treasures which are chronicled as having passed by inheritance to the Grand Duchess Vittoria, the wife of Ferdinand II. de' Medici, are the cartoon for Raphael's portrait of *Julius II.*, now in the Corsini Gallery at Florence, and the said portrait, together with a copy of it made by Titian. In view of the last entry, Gronau suggests that when Titian visited Guidobaldo II. at Urbino in the year 1545, when on his way to Rome, the latter may have commissioned him to copy the portrait of his great uncle, which was then hanging in Santa Maria del Popolo.

RAPHAEL SANTI

The fact that there is a version of the same composition in the Pitti Palace complicates the problem of identification, and critics are not in entire agreement on the question of priority. Crowe and Cavalcaselle consider the original seen by Vasari in S. Maria del Popolo to be lost, and are disposed to regard the version in the Uffizi as a copy by Penni, and that in the Pitti as by Giovanni da Udine, admitting, however, a certain priority in the former. The prevalent opinion of more recent criticism would regard its authenticity as indisputable, and on the comparison of the two versions, stylistic evidence seems equally conclusive. It possesses more of the freedom and the hesitance of original work. The structure lines of the face are stronger and more vital. The Pitti example is smoother and richer in texture, but the fire has gone from the eye and the vigour from the taut lines of the mouth. Out of the strong comes forth sweetness. To suppose that from the version in the Pitti a copyist or pupil, or even Raphael himself, could build up the figure in the Uffizi portrait is to suppose the process reversed. The technique of the version in the Pitti, with its smooth handling and its richness of colour, is not apparently inconsistent with the supposition that it may be identical with the copy executed by Titian, of which the inventory makes mention.

XVI

THE PORTRAIT OF BALDASSARE CASTIGLIONE

LOUVRE, PARIS

PIETRO Bembo in a letter written to Cardinal Bibbiena, on the nineteenth of April, 1516, eulogises the portrait which Raphael had just painted of the poet Antonio Tebaldeo, as more lifelike than any he has ever seen, declaring that so far as likeness goes, the portraits of Baldassare Castiglione and of the late Duke were merely apprentice work, in comparison with that of Tebaldeo. The passage contains all that is known about the portrait, which has disappeared, as has also that of the Duke Guidobaldo.

The portrait of Baldassare Castiglione, after many wanderings, has passed into the Louvre Collections. At the sight of its quiet, yet vibrant harmony of sober black and wheaten-grey tones, of the ineffable air of gentleness and distinction which Raphael has imparted to the features of the author of the *Perfect Courtier*, whose widely opened grey blue eyes look out with such a frank benignity, the words of Bembo's letter seem perforce to be merely magnificent hyperbole, for the reason that art could never compass such a degree of verisimilitude as should cause this likeness to seem other than a masterpiece. They serve, however, to indicate what other evidence confirms, that the portrait of Baldassare Castiglione did not stand alone; it was one of several portraits which Raphael painted of that circle of friends who took delight in social intercourse. 'Tomorrow,' wrote Bembo in a letter to Bibbiena at Fiesole six days earlier than that from which I have quoted, 'Navagero, Beazzano and I intend to revisit Tivoli with Baldassare Castiglione and Raphael . . . We shall see the new and the old and everything that is beautiful in the place.' What a company was there assembled! What a 'Conversation' Landor might have made of it!

The portraits of the two Venetian writers, Andrea Navagero and Agostino Beazzano, painted by Raphael on a single panel for their common friend Bembo, have been identified by Morelli with a work in the Doria Gallery. Of Bembo himself he had made a portrait in chalk when they had first met at Urbino, at the court of Guidobaldo. There, before Raphael's first visit to Florence, he must have met Castiglione when the latter had come from Rome to visit Guidobaldo in the autumn of 1504, and on his meeting him again at Urbino, two years later, the friendship had grown more intimate.

Castiglione, when sent on an embassy to England, bore with him Raphael's *S. George* as a present from the Duke to Henry VII., and in *The Courtier* he paid full homage to his friend's pre-eminence in art.

The friendship had deepened in Rome, whither Cas-

The Portrait of Baldassare Castiglione
Louvre, Paris

tiglione had gone soon after Raphael, at first as envoy of the Duke of Urbino at the Vatican, and then, after Francesco Maria had been deprived of his estates, he had acted in a similar capacity for the house of Gonzaga. The depth of Castiglione's interest in and sympathy with Raphael's projects is conclusively shown by the letter which Raphael wrote to him in reply to his congratulations on the *Galatea*, in which he spoke of the strain of his duties as architect of S. Peter's, of the extent of his hopes and ambitions in archæological research, and the pleasure with which he would defer to his friend's judgment in the selection of standards or types of beauty. He is known to have written to Ariosto to ask him for advice in the composition of the frescoes in the Stanza della Segnatura, and there can be no doubt that an intimate friend, such as Castiglione, was freely taken into his counsels in all these compositions. The choice of the Galatea subject may have been suggested to him by Castiglione, who had used it in a masque for the carnival at Urbino. Castiglione's despatches to Mantua show how continuous was his intimacy in the last years of Raphael's life. And of all the threnodes and laments which his death evoked, none seems so entirely a cry from the heart, as that uttered three months afterwards by Castiglione, in a letter to his mother at Mantua, on his return to Rome :—'I am well in health, but can hardly believe that I am in Rome, now that my poor Raphael is no longer here. May God keep that blessed soul.'

RAPHAEL SANTI

It was from the standpoint of long continued personal intimacy, with all its opportunities of unconscious self-revealment, that Raphael painted Castiglione's portrait, probably within the twelve months preceding the date of Bembo's reference to it. The fact seems entirely in keeping with its air of quietude. Its simplicity is only exceeded by that of the portrait of a Cardinal at Madrid, in which, as Wölfflin has said, 'clarity of drawing has perhaps reached its highest perfection.' A like tribute might be paid to the scheme of colour of the Castiglione. In the supreme economy of resources here displayed the painter has shown how complete is his mastery of his art. Diversified colour becomes an artifice in the presence of this exquisite harmony of silvery tones. It was copied by Rubens and Rembrandt. Had it ever been seen by Velasquez he would surely have been of the number. He could never then have professed his indifference to the work of Raphael. While in a sense the most modern of Raphael's works, in that it is most nearly in accord with the later ways of art, it reproduces the arrangement of the figure of the 'Mona Lisa' which Raphael also employed in the Madrid *Cardinal* and the *Donna Velata*. The slight difference in the angle of the body lends the expression of the face the vitality of the momentary. But he is now sure in his own strength, and though he uses the Leonardesque formula, he would be called 'the son, not the grandson of nature.'

The early history of the picture is somewhat con-

PORTRAIT OF BALDASSARE CASTIGLIONE

jectural. Castiglione was sent as ambassador to Madrid in 1525, and, from the esteem in which he held the picture, it may be regarded as certain that he took it with him. After his death, which occurred in 1529, it remained for some time no doubt in the possession of his family at Mantua.

Either Isabella d'Este, who greatly coveted examples of Raphael's work, and who in the year previous to his death had succeeded in obtaining from him, through Castiglione, a sketch for a monument which she wished him to erect to her husband who had just died, or if not Isabella, any of the subsequent Dukes of Mantua would eagerly embrace any opportunity that might present itself of acquiring the portrait for the Gonzaga collection. The probability that it was so acquired is the foundation of the belief that it was one of the many pictures from Mantua which passed into the collection of Charles I. in the year 1629, when, through the agency of the Duke of Buckingham, the Gonzaga collections of works of art were purchased for the king.

The fact that no mention of the picture occurs in Vanderdoort's catalogue of Charles I.'s collection is not conclusive evidence against this theory, because although Vanderdoort enumerates over five hundred pictures, this was less than half the total number, and it is certain that if the portrait ever were in the collection of Charles I., it did not remain there until its dispersal. We touch firm ground in 1639, at which date it was sold at Amsterdam, out of the collection of M. van Ussellen.

RAPHAEL SANTI

It was while the picture was at Amsterdam that Rembrandt executed the sketch of it in water-colour which is now in the Albertina. The copy by Rubens was made in all probability before the picture left Mantua, Rubens having lived there for several years at the commencement of the seventeenth century, under the patronage of Vincenzo Gonzaga, and having then made copies of other pictures.

At Van Ussellen's sale in 1639 the picture was bought by the Spanish ambassador, de Lopez. It afterwards passed into the collection of Cardinal Mazarin, and was acquired from his heirs in 1661 by Louis XIV., and then in course of time passed into the Louvre collections.

XVII

THE MADONNA DELLA SEDIA

PITTI GALLERY, FLORENCE

IT was in the added richness of his colour harmonies, due in part no doubt to his intercourse with Venetian masters, that the art of Raphael underwent most change during the period of his residence in Rome. The extent to which this is in evidence in the *Madonna della Sedia* is the primary factor in determining the date of the picture as being approximately contemporaneous with Raphael's historical frescoes in the Vatican, which form the decoration of what is known as the Stanza of Heliodorus. In the last discipleship here suggested, his power of assimilation was exercised on ground more entirely congenial to his temperament as an artist than that on which he adventured when he essayed problems, the preoccupation with which has made the works of Michelangelo and Leonardo comparatively infrequent.

Venice was the true home of realism in Italian art. The artist's primary purpose, as interpreted by her painters, is to reveal the life of the world as it is. Carpaccio's processions are its pageants; Giorgione's idyls are its romance; Titian's glowing canvases preserve in fidelity the lineaments of its actors—each with an unsurpassed delight in the colour of life, which was shared in varying degrees by all Venetian painters. The influence showed itself in Raphael's art in a deepening of tones and a richer impasto; it is at its maximum in the fresco of the *Expulsion of Heliodorus* and that of the *Mass of Bolsena*, more especially in the spectators and ceremonial figures, where the art of portraiture naturally followed on the lines of Venetian models.

It is with this new-found delight in colour for its own sake that he turns again to the familiar theme in the *Madonna della Sedia*. The two little sketches—first thoughts for the picture—on the sheet at Lille on which are the studies for the *Madonna of the House of Alba* are the only preparatory drawings known to exist. This fact, and the absence of any cartoon, may be looked upon as additional proofs of the paramount importance of colour in the artist's conception.

The line and the arrangement are in fact not immune from criticism. The relation of the further knee of the Virgin, on which the hands of S. John are resting, to the other part of the body is utterly unconvincing. Her hands are coarse and misshapen even for a contadina. The fingers of the left hand might equally serve to represent a bundle of roots. There is an excess of fatness in the leg of the infant Christ from knee to ankle. But for whatever falling off there may be from the purity of line of the Florentine Madonnas, the added richness of the colour makes amends. The face of the Virgin seems to glow with the sun of the Campagna, her golden chestnut hair to hold the sunlight in it as does that of the 'Magdalen' of Titian. Her striped shawl and head-dress form a rich harmony of contrasted tints. Her robe and the swarthy upturned face of S. John vibrate with colour. The modelling, while lacking something of the plastic firmness of the Florentine period, is exquisitely soft and rounded, with lights melting imperceptibly into shadows.

We know not whether to admire the more the tenderness and affection in the expression of the mother, or the sweet gravity in the face of the child, and the gentle placid grace with which he nestles in her arms. According to an old tradition the picture was drawn on the top of a wine cask from a group seen by Raphael in a street in Rome. The tradition may have been in origin a tribute to the simplicity and naturalness of the group. It would, however, account for that note of *genre* which characterises the picture above all the rest of the Madonnas of Raphael. Not only the striped shawl and head-dress, but the whole physiognomy of the Virgin reveals the Roman contadina. She is nothing more or less than a village mother with her children. M. Gillet defines the unique charm of the Florentine Madonnas as consisting in the fact that they are simply human. By virtue of this supreme quality the *Madonna della Sedia*, the latest in order of progressive development of that simpler motive which originated in the *Madonna del Gran Duca*, may be said to crown the whole series. It has been written of as 'this supreme picture of love, this absolute union of mother and child,' and of no other of the Madonnas would the description be so true. But in the series as a whole, while in the entire naturalness of the relation of mother and child he perfected what Giotto had begun, the type of the Madonna is, in intention, of the ideal. The look of lineage, the calm tranquillity of maiden thought of the *Madonna del Gran Duca* or *del Cardellino* express it more nearly. By contrast with such as these, the type of the *Madonna della Sedia* is of a dark-eyed southern countrywoman, with no thought but that of joy in her children.

The history of the picture is singularly uneventful. With the exception of a brief sojourn in Paris, as a result of Napoleon's plunderings of Italian art-treasures, from whence it returned in 1815, it has always, so far as record holds, formed part of the State Collections of the Medici. It is mentioned first in the year 1589, in a catalogue of the pictures in the Tribuna of the Uffizi, and was transferred some two hundred years later to the Pitti Palace, when the Gallery there was founded by the Grand Duke Ferdinand III. The fact of it having been in the Medici Collections at so early a date has given rise to the supposition that it was painted for Cardinal Giovanni de' Medici before he was elected Pope.

An unusually large number of early copies attest the importance in which the picture was held. One of these at Toulouse, seen by the painter Ingres when a boy of

The Madonna della Sedia
Pitti Gallery, Florence

THE MADONNA DELLA SEDIA

twelve, is said to have been the inception of his life-long admiration of Raphael's work, admiration which afterwards impelled him to spend eighteen years in Rome and Florence, where his style was moulded by the constant study of Raphael's masterpieces. A remark which Ingres makes concerning Raphael might serve to define the peculiar excellence of the *Madonna della Sedia*. 'Raphael,' he says, 'had so completely mastered nature and had his mind so full of her, that instead of being ruled by her, one might say that she obeyed him, and came at his command to place herself in his picture.'

XVIII

THE MADONNA DI SAN SISTO

ROYAL GALLERY, DRESDEN

A FRENCH critic has said with reference to the 'Mona Lisa,' that for wellnigh four centuries she has caused whoever looked at her to lose his head. In the presence of certain works of art which the critic feels to be supremely great his armoury fails him. So perfect, so apparently effortless are they in their utter rightness, that, as he is constrained to acknowledge,

'Words are weak,
The glory they transfuse with fitting truth to speak.'

To attempt is but to babble with rapture and astonishment. Across a vista of twenty years I trace the inception of all interest in the art of the Renaissance to the impression created by the sight of the *Madonna di San Sisto* at Dresden. After much travel in Italy I found on returning that the old reverence had scarcely changed through observation of the work of other painters. From the time of Duccio and Cimabue onwards the representation of the Madonna and Child constituted the central motive in Italian art, and just as Raphael sums up the

THE MADONNA DI SAN SISTO

tenets and gathers in the traditions of the art of Italy more completely than any other painter, so the latest of his representations of the Madonna seems, as it were, the consummation towards which all his previous attempts are seen to be stages.

The series of the Florentine Madonnas had shown a progression in realism which culminated in the intimacy of the *Madonna della Sedia,* where the motive treated is one purely of natural human feeling. After achieving this, he goes back again to ecstasy in the *Madonna and Child with Saints Sixtus and Barbara.* This return to earlier standards reveals his wellnigh infinite variety. None of his Madonnas, except perhaps the *Gran Duca,* is so entirely reverential in feeling. But what the one achieves by its deep simplicity, the other attains by subtilty of harmonious arrangement. This arrangement was apparently decided by the fact that the work was intended to serve as an altarpiece. In all the lesser Madonnas the action is complete in itself—there being a group at which the spectator looks. But here the action of the figures—as in the outstretched hand of S. Sixtus and the downward gaze of S. Barbara—has reference to the assembly of the faithful below, for whom the aged Pope is invoking the intercession of the Madonna, while on the other side, kneeling before her, S. Barbara is looking down upon them with eyes of love. The device of the parted curtain, drawn back as though it were but the unveiling of the altar, lends a natural emphasis to the arrangement. Through it we look as to a vision set in the heavens, where in the sun-girt ether float innumerable cherubs. A region where all is light.

Two cherubs in the foreground are leaning on the low sill which serves to frame the picture. The richness of vestment of Pope Sixtus and S. Barbara characterise the work of Raphael's Roman period, and there is some suggestion of Venetian influence in the rugged upturned head of the Pope and the careless freedom of the treatment of the drapery.

So in the Child the plastic firmness of modelling of Raphael's Florentine Madonnas has yielded to the softer, more entirely natural type of the *Sedia*. The Virgin has the solemnity and the tenderness of the *Madonna del Gran Duca*. The figure is one of the most perfect ever planned and executed. The lineaments bear a sufficiently close resemblance to those of the portrait of the Roman period known as *La Donna Velata* to point to the same model having served for both pictures, but while one is a portrait the other is elemental. The colouring—more subdued than is usual in pictures of the latest Roman period—retains something of the Umbrian. It has some affinity even with so professedly Peruginesque a work as the *Crucifixion*.

It was, perhaps, the comparative lowness of the tones that drew from Correggio the remark attributed to him on seeing the picture at Piacenza, 'anche io sono pittore.' The words seem to convey some suggestion of the pride that apes humility.

The genesis of the *Madonna di San Sisto* is given

THE MADONNA DI SAN SISTO

with brevity by Vasari. Raphael, he says, 'painted for the black friars of San Sisto in Piacenza, the picture for the high altar, in which was Our Lady with S. Sixtus and S. Barbara; and it was in truth a most rare and matchless work.' The position of this sentence in the order of Vasari's narrative confirms the conclusion to which all stylistic indications point, that the work belongs to the latter part of the Roman period. It is difficult to understand how so great a masterpiece by a painter so illustrious came to be executed for a monastery in a comparatively obscure town in the north of Italy, at a time when Isabella d'Este and others were in vain putting forward requests for pictures from him. Crowe and Cavalcaselle, attaching importance to what is perhaps only a mere coincidence of name, have suggested that the Cardinal of San Sisto, Antonio de' Monti, may have been requested to use his advocacy in obtaining the commission for the monks of Piacenza; they derive a possible date for the occurrence from the fact that the Cardinal, whose likeness was introduced by Raphael in the fresco in the Vatican of the *Giving of the Decretals*, was present at the meeting of Leo X. and Francis I. at Bologna. This was a ceremonial occasion which gave peace for a time to Italy. The Papal army had previously been at Piacenza, and with them was Leonardo da Vinci. A note in his manuscripts of the order of the towns between Piacenza and Bologna may be interpreted as marking his route to the latter town, where he was present at the Concordat, and made a sketch of

Aetus, the king's chamberlain. It was shortly after this that Leonardo entered the French king's service. May not his services have been invoked at Piacenza by the monks of San Sisto? In this case the journey from Piacenza to Bologna may have given him the opportunity of proceeding further with the matter, since Crowe and Cavalcaselle speak of Leonardo as accompanying Raphael from Rome to Florence and Bologna. If this could be accepted it would at once fix a probable term to the commission, by establishing the fact of Raphael's presence in Piacenza. Leonardo left Rome presumably with Giuliano de' Medici and the Papal army, in July 1515, and leaving Giuliano sick at Florence they went to Piacenza, and from there to Bologna in December, but there does not appear to be any proof of Raphael's presence, and his activity in Rome was such as to render so long an absence improbable.

Knowledge, as apart from conjecture as to the origin of the picture, begins and ends with Vasari's statement. No preparatory studies for the *Madonna di San Sisto* are known to exist. The fact enhances the probability of what the picture itself suggests—that it was the product of a single act of conception—that in it the painter's thought moved swiftly, surely, inevitably towards its predestined goal.

The picture remained at Piacenza until the year 1754, when the monks of San Sisto, blinded by the lure of avarice, were induced to sell it for 60,000 florins—the equivalent of £9000—to an agent of the Elector of

THE MADONNA DI SAN SISTO

Saxony, Augustus III., and replace it by a copy. The painter, Carlo Cesare Giovannini, has gained an unenviable notoriety from the fact of his having been the intermediary in the sale, whereby the greatest of Raphael's Madonnas passed out of Italy.

Since 1754 the picture has been in the Royal Gallery at Dresden.

XIX

THE PORTRAIT OF LEO X. WITH THE CARDINALS GIULIO DE' MEDICI AND LUDOVICO DE' ROSSI

PITTI GALLERY, FLORENCE

THERE is an Epicurean ring in the sentence used by Cardinal Giovanni de' Medici when writing on the evening of the day of the Conclave to announce to his brother Giuliano the fact that he had been chosen as successor to Julius II. 'Let us enjoy the Papacy, since God has given it to us.' The words are a key-note to the record of the reign of Leo X. They serve to call up something of the luxury and magnificence which characterised his tenure of the headship of the Church. Being a Medici—son of Lorenzo the Magnificent—it is natural that the patronage of art and song should be among the chief of the enjoyments with which he filled up the measure of his days.

With the death of Julius II. the strong hand was removed from the rudder, and to an age of ambitious statecraft succeeded one of luxury and nepotism. The change was not at first apparent. Rome had never held

The Portrait of Leo X with the Cardinals Giulio de' Medici and Ludovico de' Rossi
Pitti Gallery, Florence

THE PORTRAIT OF LEO X.

so many men of letters as were gathered at the court of Leo X., and they served as his eulogists. In the fine arts, he entered at once upon the inheritance of the vast projects of Julius II. Raphael's work in the Stanza of Heliodorus was approaching the point of completion, but it had not progressed so far but that the painter, courtier-like, could vary his design in the fresco of the meeting of Leo I. and Attila and give the lineaments of Leo X. to his predecessor. He had referred in the letter to Francia, written at the outset of his residence in Rome, to the exacting patron who allowed him no leisure; but the change of Popes brought no intermission to his activity. The decoration of room after room in the Vatican proceeded with unexampled rapidity.

He was conservator of ancient monuments and was engaged in archæological researches. He was appointed architect of S. Peter's in succession to Bramante, and was employed in various architectural projects, being one of those summoned to Florence in connection with the Pope's project for a façade to the church of San Lorenzo, the burial-place of the Medici. Amid the great number of paintings which he undertook at this period a few are distinguished by a standard of execution which is itself the most potent argument for assigning the remainder to the hands of pupils. Among these the portrait of Leo X. has a certain pre-eminence, almost akin to that possessed by the *Sistine Madonna* and the upper part of the *Transfiguration*. They are the latest of the works which may be characterised as entirely the creation of his own hand. They show that to the end he was still reaching forward to new heights in art.

The date of the picture is fixed within narrow limits by the fact that Ludovic de' Rossi, the figure on the right of the Pope, was only created a Cardinal in 1517 and died two years afterwards. It is probably the latest example of Raphael's work in portraiture. It is equally of interest as the presentment in all fidelity of the Medici Pope, and as an example of the ultimate stage of the progress of Raphael's art from symbolism to realism, shown in the difference between the imaginative conceptions of the Stanza della Segnatura and the sequence of historical compositions which followed in the other rooms of the Vatican. It contains passages of colour of a marvellous depth and richness to which the *Mass of Bolsena* affords the most conspicuous parallel. They reveal the full extent to which he had been influenced by the work of Venetian masters during his residence in Rome. But a more significant factor than these colour visions in the resultant harmony is the incidence of the light, which is rendered with such subtilty and diversity, as it plays on the flesh and the white lawn of the robes, as to produce everywhere the effect of motion. The structure and modelling of the figures of the Pope and the two cardinals his nephews go back in essential strength, dignity and mentality, to the greatest creations of his Florentine exemplars.

As in their work, so here, nothing is extenuated.

THE PORTRAIT OF LEO X.

Leo X. is represented as a short, thick-set man, with a fat, heavy face, with a large jaw, a loose mouth and full lips. The pleasures of the table would seem to have set their mark upon him. His colour is sallow and his hands are white and flabby. While the one holds a lens the other is resting upon the open page of an illuminated book. The incident may perhaps serve to recall the disclaimer of Pope Julius II. to Michelangelo. One must infer that Leo X., on the contrary, either chose to be painted with a book or acquiesced in the suggestion of Raphael, but, to do the dilettante justice, the book was one worthy of a collector. The cardinals in the background serve as foils to enhance the massive girth and general air of domination of Leo X. The portrait was painted shortly after the execution of Cardinal Petrucci who had conspired against the life of the Pope. The fact may be held accountable for a certain hardness in the expression and a vindictive look in the eyes underlying the geniality of the *bon vivant*.

The lifelike nature of the presentment has received picturesque tribute. Lanzi says that on one occasion Baldassare Turini, the Cardinal Notary, found himself approaching it with a bull and pen and ink, to obtain the Pope's signature.

Vasari emphasises its structural vitality by the remark that the figures seem round in full relief rather than rendered on a flat surface. He also does eloquent justice to the skill and detailed care displayed in its execution, in the velvety softness of the skin, the sheen of the damask of the Pope's robe, the softness of the ermine of the lining, and the absolute verisimilitude of the gold and silk ; noting also the quality of the page of miniatures, and the chasing of a silver bell 'of an indescribable beauty,' which stands beside the book on the table, and mentioning finally a ball of burnished gold on the back of the Pope's chair, which is of such brightness as to reflect the divisions of the window, the shoulders of the Pope and the walls of the room.

At the time at which Vasari wrote, the picture had passed into the possession of the Medici family at Florence. Passavant is our authority for the statement that in 1589 it hung above the entrance door of the Tribuna. It was taken to Paris in 1797 and in 1815 it was restored to the Medici Collections at Florence.

XX

THE PORTRAIT OF A LADY

UFFIZI GALLERY, FLORENCE

IT was in discussing the authenticity of this picture that Morelli referred incisively to the limitations of that science of connoisseurship of which he was the foremost exponent. 'Only charlatans and novices in the study have a name ready for every work of art.' While, therefore, controverting on what may be termed morphological grounds the traditional ascription to Raphael, he was content to call the picture merely the work of an important Florentine master, as it did not appear to afford sufficient clues to warrant attributing it with confidence to any particular master.

The tradition of Raphael's authorship has some measure of antiquity. The picture is known to have been in the Pitti Palace in 1710, there attributed to Raphael. It was afterwards taken to the Medici villa at Poggio a Capano, and was brought back to Florence in 1773 and the official ascription has never varied. Conjecture has also been busy among the records of the painter's life to discover the identity of the sitter. It was once supposed to be the portrait of Maddalena Doni, but the discovery of the two Doni portraits rendered the theory untenable. On the score of some fancied resemblance it has been styled Raphael's mother or sister. If the former, it could not possibly be the work of the painter. There is not, however, a shred of evidence, either in the picture or elsewhere, which throws any light at all on the question of identity.

The frequency in early registers of ascriptions such as this on which the tradition of Raphael's authorship rests, tends directly to impugn their value as art documents. Tradition alone cannot establish authenticity, and in this case, in the judgments of some of the foremost critical authorities, the necessary confirmation is not forthcoming from internal evidence. To review these, however cursorily, is to plunge into a conflict of opinions.

The picture is accepted as by Raphael by his two biographers—Passavant and Müntz. The former considered the surface to be so worn that the painter's touch could only still be recognised in parts, especially in the hands. To Müntz, on the contrary, the touch is everywhere apparent. He held that the picture displayed a freedom and a vigorous science in excess of that seen in the work done by Raphael during his first years in Florence, and was consequently of a later date. Venturi, on the other hand, considers it earlier than the Doni portraits, and believes that Raphael painted the same figure again, rejuvenated and idealised, in the Cumean Sibyl in the Cambio at Perugia, where he laboured for a time as assistant to Perugino. Corrado Ricci agrees with

The Portrait of a Lady
Uffizi Gallery, Florence

THE PORTRAIT OF A LADY

Müntz in assigning the work to a more mature stage of Raphael's development than that represented by the Doni portraits, and both Ricci and Müntz, and also Venturi, would see in the picture the dominating influence of Leonardo.

On the other hand, Crowe and Cavalcaselle, Berenson, Wölfflin, and Gronau are in agreement with Morelli in that they do not accept the traditional ascription of the picture to Raphael. A certain preponderance may be conceded to this consensus of opinion, but the unanimity is not of long duration. In estimating the authorship of the picture the critics fall into two groups. Crowe and Cavalcaselle and Gronau agree with Morelli that it is the work of a Florentine.

According to the first, Raphael could only have produced such a work if on coming to Florence he had surrendered the Umbrian style to assume that of a pure Florentine, and they do not consider that there is any evidence of his ever having performed a feat of this kind. Berenson, on the other hand, apparently sees enough of the Umbrian in the execution of the picture to warrant him in assigning it to Perugino, and in this attribution Wölfflin concurs, holding it to be irrefutable on account of the great affinity which the work bears to Perugino's portrait of Francesco dell' Opere in the Uffizi.

The picture certainly presents a closer stylistic analogy to what is the most impressive example of Perugino's power of interpretation than it does to any authenticated example of the work of Raphael, and in this fact the theory of Perugino's authorship finds its chief contributory support.

If, however, the picture be accepted as the work of Perugino, it reveals some accession of freedom and depth of power. It would as a consequence become necessary somewhat to extend what are usually regarded as the confines of the Peruginesque, and to recognise that the painter's association with Leonardo was more fertile in the transmission of power to interpret in quietude the deep springs of emotion than has elsewhere found expression. The scheme of colour has a general resemblance to those of Perugino, but there is a certain enhanced precision and delight in line which seems to derive directly from the Florentine masters of the Quattrocento—Ghirlandaio and the Pollaiuoli.

The apparent convergence of influences presents difficulties in the path of any definite solution, but Raphael's extraordinary adaptability and power of assimilation by contrast with the comparative homogeneity of Perugino's art have some indirect effect in reinforcing the verdict of tradition.

How, however, is it possible to reconcile with the theory of Raphael's authorship the somewhat definitely Quattrocento character of the composition, shown in the miniature-like precision of detail and firmness of structure, together with the fact that the handling reveals everywhere a suavity and maturity of touch? It has, moreover, a power to interpret emotion by contrast, with which the two Doni portraits are at best mere superficial renderings of externals, although these, as being experiments in the Leonardesque sense of atmosphere and space-gradation, are stages along the road which led to the riper humanism of the Roman work.

So while the one critic would give the Tribuna picture the priority over these by reason of its Quattrocento characteristics, others place it later because of its apparently greater maturity of power.

The latter conjecture would seem the more probable, if the circumstance of a visit from Florence to Perugia or Urbino occurred to cause a recrudescence of Quattrocento sympathies, or that the ever-nascent art returned a stage nearer to the old moorings.

But what is this other than conjecture?

CPSIA information can be obtained
at www.ICGtesting.com
Printed in the USA
LVHW060349070622
720676LV00015B/149